RED SNOW

RED SNOW

A Young Pole's Epic Search for His Family in Stalinist Russia

by

Telesfor Sobierajski
and
illustrated by him

LEO COOPER
LONDON

First published in Great Britain in 1996 by
LEO COOPER
190 Shaftesbury Avenue
London WC2H 8JL

an imprint of
Pen & Sword Books Ltd
47 Church Street
Barnsley
South Yorkshire
S70 2AS

ISBN 0 85052 500 4
A CIP record for this book is available from the British Library

Typeset by Phoenix Typesetting, Ilkley, West Yorkshire.

Printed in England by Redwood Books, Trowbridge, Wiltshire.

DEDICATION

TO MY FAMILY, ESPECIALLY MY MOTHER, WHO WAS
LEFT BEHIND

CONTENTS

Preface

There is no doubt in my mind that almost everyone has an urge to tell, or put on paper, their life experience, and it matters not whether these are happy, sad, or in some cases horrific.

Very often the reaction of a listener or a reader plays the decisive part, and then the story is told, or dies if the recipient shows signs of disbelief or boredom. I am saying this because, very early on, when I wanted to tell my story one unforgettable remark stopped me with such force that thereafter I was unwilling to talk about it for fear of ridicule.

It happened sometime in 1950. I was at work with some Englishmen when someone asked, "Where do you come from? How did you get here?" In my limited and broken English I told them about the sad times I spent in Russia. After a while one of the listeners interrupted and said that he did not believe me. This disturbed me very much. I was accused of lying. How could anyone question my years of extreme pain and suffering? What could I do to put this unexpected wrong right? I asked him to give me one good reason why I should be lying. The answer shook me even more: "Because I listen to the BBC." This I could not understand. From that moment I very rarely mentioned my past, especially to English people, for fear of being called a liar.

Time clouds the clarity of memories and on occasions thoughts of uncertainty, whether it really happened, enter one's mind, but then many vivid and unforgettable events come back, and the complete life picture becomes real.

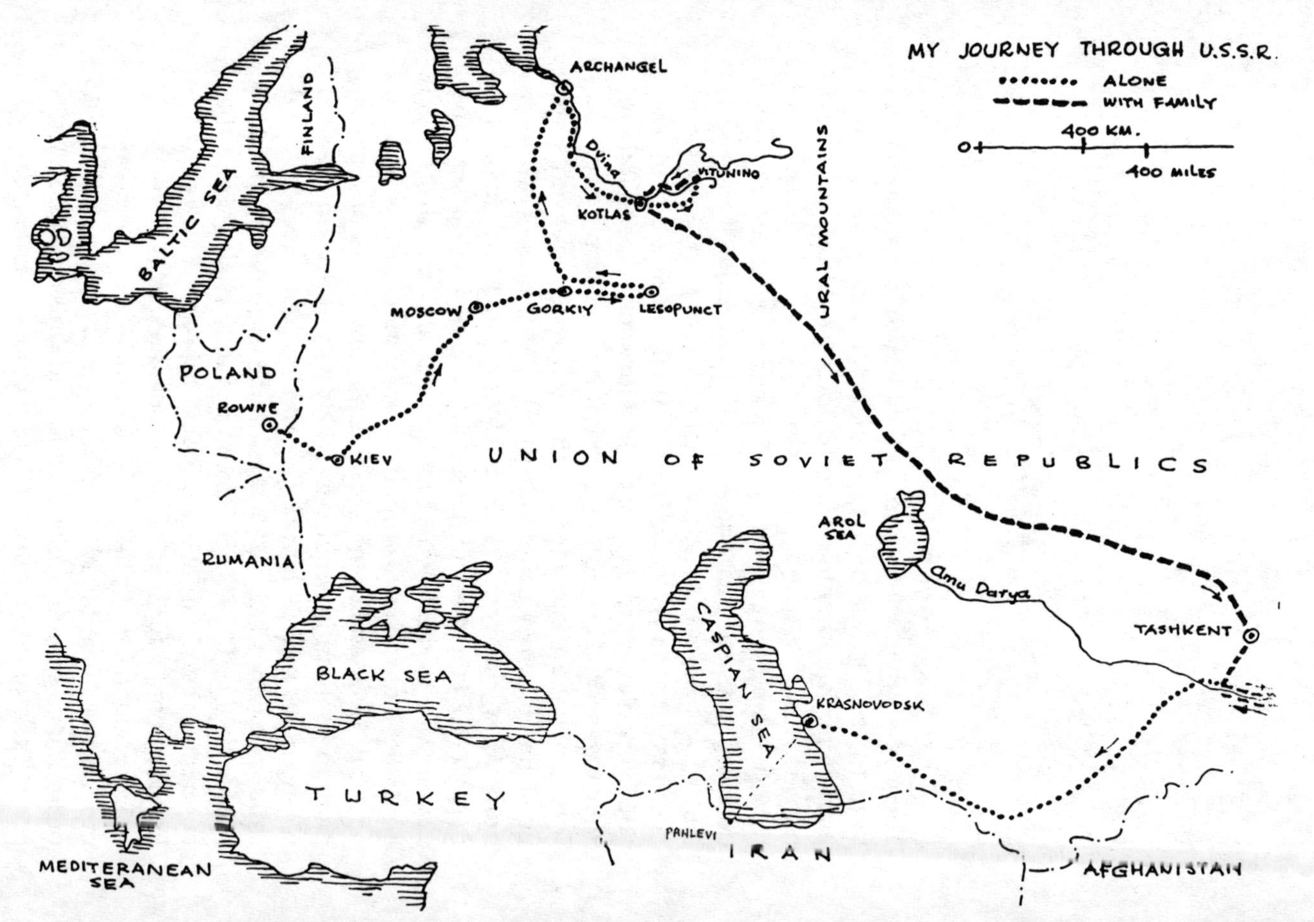

MY JOURNEY THROUGH U.S.S.R.
ALONE
WITH FAMILY
0
400 KM.
400 MILES
BALTIC SEA
FINLAND
ARCHANGEL
Dvina
VITUNINO
KOTLAS
URAL MOUNTAINS
POLAND
MOSCOW
GORKIY
LESOPUNCT
ROWNE
KIEV
UNION OF SOVIET REPUBLICS
AROL SEA
Amu Darya
RUMANIA
CASPIAN SEA
TASHKENT
BLACK SEA
KRASNOVODSK
TURKEY
PAHLEVI
IRAN
MEDITERANEAN SEA
AFGHANISTAIN

1

Early Days

I was born in September, 1925, in a small hamlet in that eastern part of Poland known as the Prypec Marshes. As the name implies the region was full of lakes, rivers and wooded marshes. After the First World War, when the Poles defeated the Red Army, the land I was born in was annexed from Russia. To Polonize the newly acquired possessions, young Poles, especially those who had taken part in the fighting, were sent to settle there; my father was one of them. He, with dozens of other young men, were given plots of land, and with financial help from the Government built their farmhouses, bought the stock and eventually married. To do that they went back west, where they were born, to find and marry their partners. When I was a young boy I often overheard the grown-ups talking of the difficulties and sheer hard work of establishing themselves as farmers, especially as many of them came from towns and had no idea of farming.

Our hamlet was very isolated, the nearest sizeable village was some 6 miles away. There you could find other Poles, otherwise all the surrounding small villages were populated by Ukrainians. The only sign of civilization was a railway 2 miles from our home with a small station. Ten miles away in the opposite direction was the River Horyn, where in later years I often fished and swam, though my first swim was in a small lake some 100 yards from my house. That lake was my constant playground. In the summer I swam there, fished,

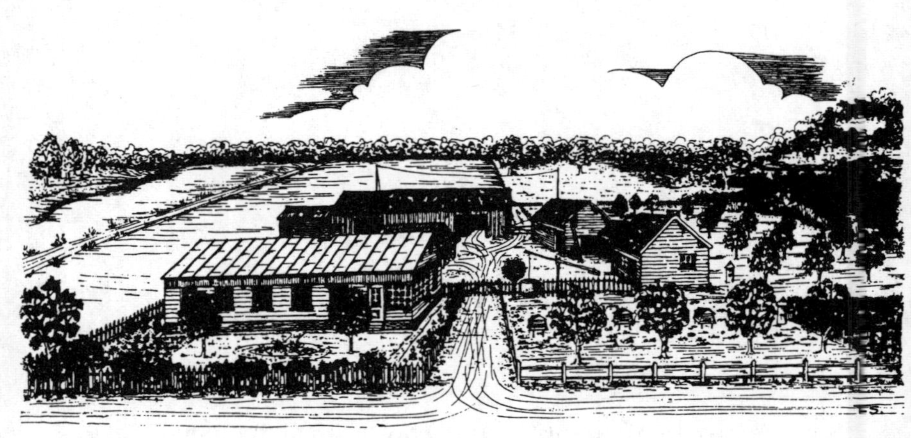

rowed my boat, and set traps for wild duck; in the winter I skated there and fished through a hole in the ice. That lake also nearly cost my life. Once, with a small axe, I set out to find a Christmas tree, and, walking across the frozen lake I spotted a nice piece of board under the ice. By cutting a hole, I thought I could recover it, but the board would only move a foot or so, so I cut another hole. Before long there were a number of holes, and of course the ice broke and I found myself in very cold water. I managed to get out and, wet and frightened, rushed home for sympathy, but got a good hiding for being so careless.

My innocent years of youth up to 1934 I spent in Chylin, the hamlet where I attended my first four years of schooling, and here was my first vivid recollection. On my way back from school, on a very warm and beautiful day, I lay in freshly cut grass and watched a lark singing above. I was very happy then.

Life was full of surprises, discoveries and joy on our farm of some sixty acres, where I roamed the woods looking for mushrooms and climbed trees, sometimes finding a bird's nest. Once I found a nest of small birds. I took one home,

put him in a cage and fed him. The bird grew up into a beautifully coloured Jay and I called him Frank. The day came when I made up my mind to let him fly, and to my great joy Frank came back to me after a while, to be fed again. For weeks we were inseparable, until one day I found him drowned in a well, and I cried at the loss of a friend. I consoled myself with other birds in years to come.

Many times, with friends, I went to the river where the world seemed large, never to be conquered. Here there was no one to spoil our youthful dreams; we were the pioneers discovering the wilderness. We were, we thought, the first to walk in those woods, meadows, and by the beautiful banks of the wide river: Here we learned to fish, which we took very seriously, for it also provided meals at home. Since money was in short supply, we made our own fishing lines from horses' tails, preferably white. The hair was rolled and tied together to make a line; a straight tree branch became a rod and bird feathers made a good float. The only item we

had to buy was a hook, and our parents provided us with them. Thus equipped with earthworms as bait, we spent numerous days mainly fishing, sometimes swimming, and generally messing about by the river. Those were wonderful days of carefree, uncomplicated life on the farm, except for times when you were told to mind the cows or horses or even weed the garden.

In 1935, to further my education, I had to go to the little town of Wysock to attend school there for the next two years, to complete six years of compulsory education. I lodged with a Jewish family, where my older sister was already living, being one year older. Gone were the carefree days and open spaces. Here I was among strangers. How I looked forward to the school holidays when I could return to my small world centred around the lake. Most memorable was the spingtime, when the river broke its banks, and flooded the surrounding meadows to form one large expanse of water between

Wysock and Chylin. The only way to get across was to hire a rowing boat; a man would ferry you from one side to the other against a fast-flowing current. I always found the journey exciting. It lasted more or less an hour on exceptionally clear water, through which you could see fast-moving fish darting through tall swaying grass.

In winter I often skated on the river on my homemade skates. Later on I was the proud owner of new shining steel skates, I think they were made in Sheffield. Some winters were very severe and travel became hazardous. Then my father would come with me on a horse-drawn sledge. To keep warm, bricks would be heated up, wrapped up in rags and placed near the feet.

By now the family was complete. My mother was always there when I was looking for love and comfort, or sometimes protection when threatened with punishment. She was very religious and, although we did not have a church, she often joined other women for prayer and singing. When the gathering happened in our house I heard, for the first time, readings from the Bible which I found very mysterious, sometimes even threatening. Only when the conversation turned to old Polish fables was I all ears. My father, I always felt, gave me a sense of security, strongly mixed with discipline, and what he said was never challenged. I rarely saw him during the summer, except in the evenings when he occasionally took us around, proudly showing his orchard, beehives, livestock and acres of grain. More often than not, we finished near my beloved lake. Only winter found us together when he showed interest in my schooling and hobbies. He made my first ice skates and skis, and I soon mastered the art of staying vertical.

There were four of us children, my elder sister Lucja and two younger sisters, Joanna and Jagoda. Having three girls as immediate friends somehow did not work out. They played different games; they did not fish and did not take any interest in birds. Only later did the brother/sister relationship develop.

My schooldays in Wysock came to an end in 1938. Little did I know that the summer holiday that year would be the last happy and peaceful one I would spend there. By now I took a more active part in the farm activities. My father taught me ploughing, mowing, threshing and even manure-spreading: I cannot say all this appealed to me, but I was pleased when the elders nodded their heads in approval. There were times at the end of the day when all of us, covered in dust and dirt, would make our way to the river for a general clean up and swim. There we often met other families with similar ideas. Bathing was done in the nude, but in separate groups: men, women and children.

That summer I knew my future schooling would be discussed and when the day arrived my ideas of becoming a soldier or an airman were quickly dismissed. I was going to Gimnazjum (grammar school) and that was that! The nearest grammar school was approximately two hundred miles away in a town called Pinsk on the Prypec River. Not long after, father, two elder sisters and myself boarded a train and set out on what was, to me, a pleasant and exciting journey. The town, with its cobbled streets and rows of brick buildings was much larger than I imagined. I found it foreboding and menacing. This feeling never left me while I was there. After a stop at a small restaurant, we made our way to a large three-storey brick building, with lots of windows, not very far from the station. Inside we found a number of boys with their families. After various interviews and a short entrance exam-ination, my father proudly announced that I had been accepted as a boarding student.

Home again for a short break, and then I was on my way back to Pinsk to begin my studies. The boarding house was a long one-storey building, occupied mostly by boys, with a securely separated front portion for girl students. Time was allocated for different activities and rigorously observed. Only once a week were we allowed to go to town, and only then if one's behaviour was up to scratch. My visits were concen-trated mostly around the open spaces along the river, where from time to time armoured Navy boats sailed by. Occasionally we played games in nearby fields. Otherwise my time was spent on studies. The school year went by very slowly. There were rumours of conflict with Germany regarding certain "Corridors", which I ignored, convinced that Germany would not dare to attack, as we were far too strong. We were invincible, of that I was convinced.

Summer vacation again, but the year was 1939 and obviously there was something seriously wrong. I could see and hear grown-ups with troubled faces constantly discussing in whispered voices uncertain times ahead. Beautiful weather brought the harvest sooner than expected and by now I played a useful part, though towards the end I was puzzled when my parents selected certain fruits of their labour and hid them in different parts of the farm; some was even buried underground.

The threat of war became very real when I noticed our neighbours looking at a piece of paper stuck on a telegraph pole. It was a general mobilization poster informing certain ages of men to report for Army duty. Not long after a family gathering was arranged and father told us he would be leaving us. Then followed a long conversation between my parents. Of course we promised to be helpful and good while he was away. Towards the evening sad goodbyes were said with great emotion and tears, I promised myself to become the protector of my mother and three sisters in these troubled times.

2

War and 10 February

Where were you on the day war began? What were you doing? I wish there was something eventful to recall. No doubt I was around the farm with the family busy with everyday duties. Since my father left I tried very hard to help, usually without my mother knowing what I was up to. I made a trough for the chickens to feed in and proudly showed it to my mother; I mended fences, cut the grass around the house and oiled the farm machinery. My mother, though very pleased by my efforts, asked me to consult her in future. "Why don't you go and kill some chickens?" she asked. Of course I would, no problem, but nothing is as easy as it looks. It took me a while to catch them, then hold them by their legs with one hand and cut their head off with an axe. To this day I see them jumping about without their heads!

There was no visible sign of any military action until I was asked one day to go to one of the neighbours on some errand: On my way through a wooded area I heard the distant drone of a plane. Running towards a clearing to have a better view, I heard a number of explosions. This stopped me in my tracks and suddenly I saw him. This is my second vivid recollection. Running back very fast, hiding behind a tree trunk, hardly daring to look, I was very very frightened.

I found out later that the plane was flying over the railway line and had dropped a few bombs, without much damage.

We received some letters from my father informing us that

he was posted to Stolin, a town some thirty miles away. Mother decided to visit him, but before going, we had to get some money, as we were running low, so she thought that we ought to collect our apples and sell them. With the help of our farmhand, we set out with sacks full of apples for his village. In my ignorance I imagined we would be welcomed and easily sell our wares. What we met was suspicion, abuse and menacing crowds around us. Our farmhand suggested we had better go home, which we did with practically no sales. This unpleasant experience taught me that there was little affection between Poles and Ukrainians.

Shortly after, early one morning, the whole family set out for Stolin in a horsecart. The journey was mainly across the meadows; only nearer the town did the road improve, being made out of concrete blocks, making our cart shake, accompanied by an ear-splitting noise. On arrival, our father greeted us warmly and I thought he looked rather smart in his Army uniform. After lots of questions and answers from both sides, he told us he was here to guard a railway bridge over Prypec River. He took me to the bridge and showed me the machine-gun emplacement. While we were saying our goodbyes my mother mentioned the shortage of money and our unsuccessful apple sale. We were told to contact a Jewish trader in Wysock who could help us, but never to go to villages again.

Signs of war came to me while ploughing the fields. I was disturbed by a plane travelling at some speed, being chased by a smaller plane behind. This time I had no chance of hiding. I just stood there petrified, holding the panicking horses. I heard some gunfire. Fascinated, I watched the bigger plane disappear over the horizon at a speed not matched by the smaller plane, which I presumed was ours.

As days went by more and more people would come to our house asking for food and lodgings; they came by train, on bicycles, but mostly on foot. They were refugees from western Poland running away from the advancing German Army. Many evenings we listened to their distressing stories of the German onslaught and their escape, leaving behind their homes and possessions. One group stayed with us longer than the others because they came from the town where my mother was born. Among them were two boys on bicycles. Here was my chance to master the two-wheeler which had eluded me up to now. To my joy, it did not take me long and there was no stopping me. I had to go everywhere to show off my latest accomplishment.

For a number of years we had had a crystal radio with a high aerial spanning the farmyard, and by putting on the earphones and jabbing the crystal with silver coil with a bit of luck I could find various radio stations. Most of the news was obtained that way, though programmes were often interrupted by mysterious messages. I suspected they were coded orders to the Army. Overall, the news from the front was not encouraging, but we were assured that there was still hope when our fighting men had regrouped in the East.

On the same earphones we received reports of the Russian invasion. This distressed me greatly. In my mind there was no greater evil than Communist Russia. This prejudice was drummed into me very early on from history lessons and full-colour comic books wherein the Russian Commissar was presented as a red devil. We were to learn the truth later, but at the time the Red Army's pretext for crossing our border was to liberate us from the capitalists who were exploiting the working masses, and also to stop the German Army occupying our country.

September, 1939, was for me and my family one of the most unforgettable months in our lives: war in the West, invasion from the East and, to top it all, my father was not there to give us strength and comfort. There was depression everywhere, and near panic in our small settlement, now in most cases occupied only by women and children. My three best friends, boys of my age, eagerly discussed the situation, and specifically the danger to our families. We agreed to search our homes for guns and such like, but what we were going to do with them was not very clear. Some of them already knew where their fathers kept their guns. I had no such knowledge, though I promised to do my best. Imagine my embarrassment when next some of us met and I had only an old rusted sabre to declare!

Our railway line was very much a part of our lives. We would run to meet oncoming trains and would often lay metal objects on the tracks and collect them later, completely flattened. With the news of the invasion from the East, we noticed a considerable increase in traffic. This, of course, had to be investigated. My best friend, Jerzyk, lived less than 100 yards from the line. From there we could easily meet all the trains, but what we saw made us angry: the trains were full of Red Army soldiers. In our minds all soldiers wore smart uniforms, but the ones on the train were nothing like that. The uniforms, headwear and boots differed as though collected at random, and they wore their shirts outside their trousers, tied with belts or ropes, giving the impression of a very primitive army. We looked on silently, not waving hands as we normally did. Instead we spat on the ground in disgust.

The end of September brought a ray of light into our lives when, waking up one morning, I saw my father. When the initial excitement was over, we heard how the military post where he was stationed had been abandoned before the approaching invaders. Surrender to the Russians was out of the question. The war in the West was practically over and the Commandant advised his men to go home any way they could. He gave a warning that, if caught in uniform, Russians would at best intern them as POWs, but if caught by bands of local militia they would certainly be shot. My father travelled through forests, mostly by night, and rested during the daytime.

During his absence the farm had not exactly been neglected, but badly required his immediate attention, not only his hands, but also his knowledge. We worked very hard. Apart from farm chores, there was honey to be collected, a pig to be killed which provided us with bacon and smoked sausages, and again I noted some of this produce being hidden. To make matters worse, our farmhands were going back to their villages. When asked why, no clear answer was given, but we knew. We were aware of the new régime's ideology. Slogans proclaimed the new status of the working classes. They were no longer to be exploited by people like us. We were the enemies of the State. We were capitalists, bourgeoisie, "Kulaks" or worse. Now everybody was equal, there were no private possessions. Whatever you own is just as much yours as mine, and above all there is no God!

It did not come as a great surprise when the refugees from the West decided to return home, telling us, rightly or wrongly, that at least Germany was a civilized nation and their occupation would be more bearable. We parted with mixed feelings. We were sorry to see them go, for they were company and helpful, especially while my father was away.

Being so isolated had its advantages. There was no immediate presence of our "liberators"; only visits from the local militia, made up of Ukrainians, disturbed our tense and uneasy lives. What was their purpose we could only imagine and this we viewed with foreboding. In spite of this, my parents thought that, whatever our future, their children's education should not suffer. Somehow they found out that the Gimnazjum in Pinsk was going to re-open and I was going there for my second year. Although I had only celebrated my fourteenth birthday a few weeks earlier, I tried my best to change their minds and let me stay. But with heavy heart I realized that I was again to be parted from that safe little world.

Preparations were made for my departure and I was given a new school uniform inside which, without anyone knowing, I pinned the Polish white eagle emblem which I had removed from my father's military hat. This I imagined would be my patriotic identity when, with other boys, I would form a secret organization in time to fight our occupiers. I had no doubt it would happen, for I read about it in many books. Polish literature is full of the brave exploits of young men fighting the enemy through the history of our nation. Not long ago my father had fought Austrians and Russians to regain our independence, which we had lost a hundred years earlier.

With my head full of these dreams, it made my going away somewhat more bearable.

As soon as I boarded the train with my father I knew it was going to be an anticlimax. The carriages were crowded, dirty and draughty; many windows were broken and the toilets were unusable. On our way we passed open trains full of drab and shabby-looking soldiers of the Red Army. We made very slow progress and eventually arrived in Pinsk only to find that the boarding house I had stayed in before was closed. There was nothing to do but find private lodgings. This we did, but it took us well into the evening and, being so late, my father stayed with me overnight and returned home the next day. The house was quite near the school, not very big, in a narrow street and occupied by a middle-aged woman with a daughter much older than myself.

The very first day at school – it must have been late October – I knew I was going to hate it. The building was the same, but inside there was pure confusion – crowds of girls and boys moving aimlessly from room to room. I expected an increase of students, since the new régime proclaimed that education was free, whereas before the school was fee-paying, but what I encountered was chaos. The old Headmaster had been replaced and the newcomer definitely resembled a "Commissar". In the classrooms pictures of Stalin and Lenin were predominantly displayed; classes were over-crowded; nobody seemed to care whether you had a seat, or whether you were there at all. We were told that this was the beginning of a new era and that, given time, matters would improve. Worst of all, I could not find my friends from the previous year, and even those I knew behaved oddly. Groups would gather in the yard or corridors, talking in whispers and looking suspiciously at others. My dream of secret meetings, planning the downfall of the enemy, was rapidly disappearing and I kept my white eagle well under cover.

The townspeople appeared to be stunned and subdued. There were no greetings or smiles; people walked with their heads bowed. Maybe, I thought, the masses of soldiers with their grotesque peaked hats and long bayonets on their rifles had that effect on them. Most of the churches were closed with armed guards outside, used now as barracks. Occasionally an amusing incident would break the tension, such as seeing a Russian soldier proudly displaying three or four watches strapped to each arm. Or a joke. When asked, "Have you oranges in your country?" the soldier would reply, "In the Soviet Union there are many factories producing oranges."

Weeks went by, school was as disorganized as before and lessons rarely caught my attention. Visits to the centre of town I did not find interesting. A few times I went to the cinema where only Russian films were shown. The films I saw dealt with life on a *"Kolchoz"* (a kind of co-operative farm) or a Russian revolution, and of course the "glorious" Red Army, most of which I knew to be pure propaganda, but I must say I like Russian folk songs, and to this day I have a soft spot for them.

Winter came and I was on my way home for the Christmas break, again on a cold, dirty, draughty train, but I had a warm welcome from my family. They were eager to know about the school, my lodgings and the situation in the town, in return I heard from them disturbing news of bands of Ukrainians roaming the district, robbing and, in some cases, killing people. Even so, we were going to have a good Christmas. My father's sister's family and her three children were invited to celebrate the all-important Christmas Eve. They had a small holding which my father had given them some years ago and lived only a couple of hundred yards from us. There was a Christmas tree, presents, carol singing, games and some tears, ending with a prayer for a better future.

Far too soon we were saying goodbye. What none of us realized was that it would be a long and heartbreaking period before we were together again.

3

On My Own

Back in Pinsk not much had changed, my landlady complaining all the time about food shortages and long queues. School lessons, I detected, were more and more impregnated with communist propaganda, but classrooms were not so crowded. I kept close contact with my family, writing at least one letter per week, and received the same from my parents. Now and then my mother would send me a food parcel, for which I was very grateful, especially for the home-made chocolate. There were a lot of rumours about the Polish Army still fighting in large forests, and that the Western Powers – France and England – were coming to their aid or that parts of the Polish Army were being reorganized in Romania and would soon be ready to fight back. There were rumours of people taken away from their homes and transported somewhere, no one knew where. This did not unduly trouble me, but when I did not receive a letter from home for longer than I thought reasonable I began to worry.

Towards the end of February I thought it better to go home, just for a break. I would be back as soon as I had seen that they were all right. With that in mind, I did not bother to take much with me, just a suitcase with some clothes for my mother to wash, an overcoat with a warm hat and a yellow scarf. Thus equipped, I set out on my journey home. The train made slow progress through the deep snow drifts, but gradually we were nearing my station. I was ready near the

JUMPING OFF THE TRAIN

door. To my horror the train did not stop. Panic overtook me. What was I to do? I opened the window, staring at the disappearing station. I decided I must jump. Selecting what I was convinced was the deepest snow drift, I opened the door, threw my suitcase out and jumped.

Luckily I was right. The snow was deep and soft, and covered me completely. It took a while to get out and collect my suitcase, and then I was on my way. It was early afternoon, the weather was cold and windy with an occasional snow shower. There was no need to go back to the station. I knew there was no one waiting for me. I brushed the snow off as best I could and prepared myself for approximately 10 miles of walking. The roads I knew were now unrecognizable, lost under the thick snow, except for the freshly made tracks of the train, which I decided to follow in the direction of my hamlet. By now I felt miserable and cold and the only consolation was that soon I would come to the first house, where my friend Juzek lived. There I would stop for a while to get warm and after only 3 more miles I would be home. Approaching my friend's house I was puzzled to see no smoke coming from the chimney, but I pressed on. Coming nearer I could see no signs of footprints near the front door and all the windows were frozen over. Maybe they are away, I thought, so I had a short rest and went on again. There were two other houses I had to pass on my way and, since there was no sign of smoke from either of them, I hurried forward with my heart beating fast. Now I came to the end of the high ground and there in a shallow valley I could see my home, and thank God the chimney was smoking. I forgot I was freezing. I rushed on through the small woods, over a bridge near my lake, turned left, another 50 yards and I was there. Surely by now someone should see me through the window and would come outside to greet me, but no one was there. Maybe they are sitting round the stove keeping warm, I thought. I opened the gate to the farmyard. Things did not look right; the yard looked untidy. Normally there were paths dug out of the snow to the stables and cowsheds, but there were none. However, I heard voices and laughter inside. There was something wrong, I was convinced. With trembling hands I opened the door. What I saw I shall never forget: Crowds of men and women, strangers to me, sitting around the table with plates of scrambled eggs. I stood there and cried.

Presently the door from our sitting room opened and a man walked in. I recognized him as one of our neighbours' farmhands. I did not move; I had no words to speak. I did not ask any questions, for already I knew the answer to the most important question: Where is my family? He said, "Your family were taken away by Russians." He did not know where. "But your uncle and aunt are still here." He suggested that I go and see them, but before I went he suggested I might want to have a look around the house. This was rather unexpected, but, still without a word, I walked into our sitting room. The room was dirty and practically empty, except for a couch against the far wall and a bookcase behind the open

door. I did not go any further. Silently, with great sorrow and tears in my eyes, I walked out and closed the door behind me for the last time.

In a daze, I walked towards my aunt and uncle's house. Once inside tears and questions came from all directions, but the only thing I wanted to know was what had happened to my family. I had forgotten that I was hungry, but my aunt had not. While I was eating, and long after that I listened to the events, as they knew them, of the night of 10 February, 1940. Apparently, a week or so before that fateful day, my father had had a visit from a Russian military man, who enquired into his background. He was offered some hospitality, including a certain amount of vodka which he accepted, and, before leaving, he dropped hints which my father took to be a warning that he and his family might be rehoused. These fears he confirmed to my aunt, and at the same time decided to get some food such as bacon, honey and dried bread ready just in case.

That night, a few hours after midnight, they were woken up by an impatient knocking on the door. My aunt opened

the door to find my mother standing there, explaining that they were being taken away and, pointing to the horse-drawn sleighs on the road, she ran back to catch up with the family. "Where are you going?" my aunt shouted. "We do not know," came the answer. She could just see four or five sleighs surrounded by soldiers on horseback. By this time the whole family was at the door, staring in amazement and waving, with very little response from the convoy disappearing into the distance.

There was no sleep that night. They sat there, hardly comprehending what had happened. In the morning they discovered that other neighbouring houses were also empty. As they were wondering what to do, they noticed other sleighs coming from all directions. Driving them were previously employed farmhands. They said they had come to look after the livestock, but what they did was to rob and steal whatever they could take. Some of them returned from where they came, some stayed behind to celebrate their newly acquired power. There was no need to ask who informed them of what would be happening on 10 February, 1940.

The most heartbreaking details of that night I was to find out later, much later.

Why had they not taken my aunt and uncle away, I wondered. My uncle had given some thought to this question; he explained that all the original settlers had been removed and only relatives with smallholdings remained, and these were few. Someone locally, who knew our history, must have prepared the list. Nobody knew it at the time, but that night the same fate overtook thousands and thousands of Polish families living in Russian-occupied Poland.

My short stay was interrupted by a military man who knew of my whereabouts. He had most likely been informed by the crowd I had seen in my house. His purpose, he said, was to collect and deliver me to the police station in Wysock from where I would be taken to join my family. My aunt and uncle would not hear of it; I was going to stay with them. The argument went on for a while, but in my heart I knew I would go. Although I did not realize it at the time, it was definitely the most momentous decision I had taken in my short life. Whether I had a choice I never knew, but the desire of a fourteen-year-old child to be with his family is an overwhelming one.

When she saw my meagre possessions my aunt was astounded by what little I had, and in a hurry gathered a few things, including a quilt which she wrapped around my suitcase and tied with string. For these gifts, in days to come, I was exceptionally grateful. Emotional goodbyes were said, particularly from my aunt who squeezed some money into my hand and blessed me on my way

Not much was said during the ride to Wysock. I was absorbed by thoughts of what had happened and of what lay ahead. It occurred to me that maybe my white eagle, still with me, would not be appreciated if found by my captors. After some thought, I put my hand inside my jacket pocket, unpinned the eagle and dropped it over the side into the

snow. During my short stay at the station (only a few days) I was kept under supervision, answered some questions and was promised that it would not be long before I would be with my family. This cheered me up a lot. I was eager to move and when a policeman came and told me he would be taking me to a town where others in similar circumstances were being assembled I was only too willing to go. He did not name the town. I still believed and hoped that my family was somewhere in Poland.

The weather had worsened at the beginning of March. We made our way to the railway station. Trains had not improved as we boarded a crowded and dirty carriage and found a space in a corner where I sat down on my suitcase. I was closely guarded. The policeman went with me everywhere I went as we travelled south. Not knowing our destination I was ready to get off every time the train stopped, but it was not to be until we reached Rowne, a town some 250 miles from my home. There he handed me over to the dreaded N.K.V.D. It was late in the evening and I was put into a very small room with a bunk bed where I spent the night. The next day I was called in front of one of the Commissars, where I recited my life story staring at a big portrait of Stalin behind his desk. We spoke in Russian, a language I had no difficulties with, since I knew Ukrainian, which I learned at home talking to farmhands and boys at school. Knowing both languages, Russian was comparatively easy, and I also had some lessons at school in Pinsk.

Back in the small room, I hoped someone would join me to occupy the upper bunk, someone I could talk to and share my troubles. No one came and I spent the second night on my own. In the morning I was transported by lorry to a large building which I recognized as a synagogue. The room inside was large and high, with intermediate columns, balcony and timber floor. Near the door there was a table and chair, where a soldier sat with a rifle by his side. The floor was covered with straw mattresses laid in rows against the wall and two rows in the middle. Most of the places near the walls were occupied, while the middle rows were practically empty. The soldier got up and told me to find myself a place. Not seeing any familiar faces, I selected a vacant mattress at a distance from the others, put my suitcase down and sat on it. There was not much movement except for small children running around. People sat on their mattresses talking in whispers. I began to look around. There were men, women and children of all ages, but I felt there was something odd. I could not put my finger on what.

Hours went by and I felt very lonely and abandoned, still in my school uniform, when a rather pretty woman with a slim figure and bushy dark hair came to me. She was about my mother's age. I briefly told how I came to be here. She put her hand on my shoulder and asked me to come and join her at the end of the row where she was with her daughter, slightly younger than myself, on the plump side and very quiet. From that moment on I was adopted. This pleased me greatly. She said that I reminded her of her son, who also

attended the Gimnazjum and had the same uniform. Her husband had been taken from their home on 10 February, 1940, while she was away with her daughter visiting relatives. She told me that all the people in the synagogue were only parts of families. Now I understood why I felt there was something odd: there was not one complete family.

Daily, at no regular intervals, more people joined us, coming individually and in groups; the hall was getting full. They came from various parts of Poland, all with the hope of being re-united with the rest of their families, though nobody knew where they were. Food was delivered twice daily, mostly soup and bread, and distributed under strict control of the guard. He selected some women to help him with this chore, among them my adopted mother. I suspected he liked her and consequently our share did not lack quantity, but fell very short on quality. At this early stage a lot of people still

23

had some provisions which they had brought with them and this amply supplemented the food given.

We were not allowed to leave the premises, which were getting more crowded every day, and there was very little to do. So it came as a great surprise when my guardian asked me if I wanted to go to town and see a film with her daughter. Without hesitation I said yes, but how? She said she would speak to our guard. This she did. I watched them: my guardian, using her charm, which she had in abundance, with a constant smile on her face and in deep conversation. Nodding her head on her way back, I knew she had succeeded. She told us to get ready and she would lead us outside, leaving us to find our way into the town. Snow was everywhere and the pavements were rather slippery as we made our way down the hill. Not long after, we came to a large square with tall brick buildings on all sides, covered in red coloured placards with white letters all written in Russian. I could hardly believe my eyes when I read them. They were proclaiming the benefits of communism, welcoming the glorious Red Army, and calling all working people to unite, all punctuated with the hammer and sickle. Gazing at these enthusiastic pronouncements, I could not imagine they represented the true feeling of my people. I was sure they were made and displayed by the Russians themselves.

The film we saw was about the Russian Revolution, with a lot of fighting, singing and flag-waving. When we came out, walking back to the synagogue it occurred to me that if I wanted to escape, now was the time. This at first seemed very tempting but where would I go? What would I do? And had I forgotten why I was there?

4

East To Nowhere

March was a week or so old and the synagogue was full when one morning we were awakened by the noise of lorries outside. In no time the doors opened and in walked a party of Russian soldiers with peaked hats and long bayonets, ordering us to get ready to leave. Though we were expecting to be moved, when it came the hall was suddenly alive with raised voices, running feet and clicks of closing suitcases. Outside soldiers watched us as we climbed into the lorries. There was some commotion as friendships had now been formed and people did not want to be separated. Our trio managed to stay together.

Escorted by the Red Army, we arrived at a railway siding and stopped at a line of several cattle trucks with sliding doors open, tiny high level windows covered with barbed wire and immediately noticeable metal flues sticking out through the roof. At first disbelief all around, followed by questions: Is this transport for us? Are we all going together? Where are we going? These questions preoccupied our conversation for some time, but there were no answers.

We got off the lorries and were led towards the wagons. Keeping close together the three of us climbed inside. Surely there was no more room, we thought, but still they came, pushed and prodded by the soldiers until there were sixty or so of us. Then, bang! click! The door was closed and locked. We were in darkness, except for the dim light

EAST TO NOWHERE

coming through the small barbed-wire windows.

Near panic was avoided when a tall, fat man shouted over everybody's cries to shut up, look around and consider as soberly as possible our predicament. There were faint cries from a few small children and babies. When our eyes became acclimatized what we saw horrified us. At each end of the wagon there were two tiers of full-width timber boards as our sleeping accommodation. The middle part had a cast-iron heating stove in the centre with some coal and logs. We wondered what was the purpose of the hole in the floor about 12" in diameter. We did not have to wait long to realize that it was our toilet. Disorientated and terrified, especially the young children, we were comforted by the tall, fat man who, after a short speech, made some useful suggestions, which without a protest we followed. Our possessions were pushed to the end of the boarded bunks and, to vacate the middle portion,

26

we climbed onto the beds in such a way as to keep the children away from the draughty sides of the wagon. Slowly some kind of order and comfort was achieved. Someone lit the fire, someone else put up a kind of curtain around the hole in the floor. Our trio settled down on the upper bunk, bunched together like sardines. After all, life goes on.

Departure was not as soon as we thought. We stayed in Rowne for a couple of days. On occasion the door would open and chosen people would be allowed out under escort to collect food; my guardian was always one of the first to volunteer. The shortage of suitable containers for carrying food was acute, so one of the most treasured possessions was a tin can with a wire handle, and the bigger the better.

Finally the day came when our wagons were hitched to a goods train and we were on the move. Those near the small windows shouted out the names of the stations we were passing. After a while it became obvious that we were going east and it would not be long before we would be crossing the Polish/Russian border. At that moment emotions were let loose, with tears, sobs and cries to God. Someone started singing the Polish anthem, but few took it up. Then uneasy silence in the unknown land.

Names of stations were still called out, but hardly anyone took notice. Only the monotonous sound of wagon wheels riding over the railway lines filled the truck. This sound never displeased me and I found in it unexplained comfort. Most of my time I spent on the boards. Only when nature's call forced me did I go down, which I did not find easy. Were it not for the cracks in the walls, open windows and the speed of the train, the air inside could have been unbearable when the hole was in use. We restrained from using this primitive facility while the train was stationary. Now and then I would look through a barbed wire window, only to see vast lands covered in snow, interrupted by railway stations, many overshadowed by huge statues of Stalin.

We stopped in stations small and large, mainly to be hitched to a different train, sometimes for a few minutes, but often for hours. During long stays we were given soup and

often some bread, but always *kipiatock*, which was boiled water. Practically every station had it, usually at the end of the platform. There you found a tap where *kipiatock* was collected not only by us, but also by Russian travellers, and used for many purposes. Adding whatever you still had made a soup, or drinking it as one would drink tea, especially if there was chicory, which you kept in your mouth and let the *kipiatock* swill over it before swallowing. A lot of cooking was done on the round stove which was only 18" in diameter. This operation proved to be very dangerous and caused a number of bitter arguments. Dangerous, because there was no way of knowing when the train would suddenly stop or move forward. Pans had to be hand-held and even that precaution was not always successful, as a person would be thrown off balance spilling the contents at best on the floor, or at worst over herself, as women mainly did the cooking. Quarrelling broke out when someone tried to jump the queue or took too long preparing the food.

The further inland we went the less strict was the escort, the groups leaving the train became bigger and the people left behind were allowed, now and then, to leave the wagon. When this occurred we would scrounge anything that was useful to us – coal, wood and, of course, food. I was beginning to learn how to steal, but my adopted mother was best at it; many times she came back with something extra.

It took us over a week to travel from Rowne, through Kiev, to Moscow. During this time, apart from colds, diarrhoea and other ailments, we kept healthy, although I overheard concern expressed about a baby on the opposite bunker. When we stopped on the outskirts of Moscow we anxiously wondered which direction the train would take and whether we would still be together. We did not have to wait long, our tracks were going east again, through Gorky towards the Ural Mountains.

Stress and strain were by now showing. There were more quarrels; friendships ended and threats were exchanged, and there were lice. In no time at all we were all infested with them; search and destroy was an everyday occurrence. First your hair was examined by a relative or a friend, then your clothing, especially along the seams, and the successful hunt was announced by a faint click. This meant that a louse was found, squeezed between the nails of the thumbs, and killed. Hard as we tried to get rid of them, we could not. In the end we realized we were losing the battle.

Leaving Gorky behind, still travelling east, I heard whispers that a baby had died and only then I recognized sounds of sobbing and the words of comfort. Although we were moving, people were knocking on the doors shouting the bad news. Not until we stopped at a small station was the commotion heard by the soldiers escorting us. The door opened and, after prolonged arguments, the baby was wrapped up in a white cloth and taken away. Maybe we had already reached such depth of despair that this sad event did not have the effect it deserved; not even the remark by someone who was looking through the window that, while we were moving, a bundle resembling the one taken away only minutes ago was thrown from the train into the snow.

Fewer and fewer stations, more and more snow-covered spaces, until we reached a small town by the peculiar name of Suhobezvodnaya meaning literary "dry without water." Somehow we felt we were nearing the end of our travels. We were pushed into a dead-end line and the doors were opened and we were allowed out. It was only a brief stay, for a small railway engine with a tall flat funnel belching out thick black smoke was soon hitched to our wagons. We were again moving, through what seemed like never-ending woodland, with a narrow path cleared for a single railway line. We were convinced that our destination was near as this was no longer a main line; there were no other wagons except ours and we had no military escort. The atmosphere turned very sombre and speculations were very pessimistic. Surely we could not all be so lucky that our families would be here, but at least we hoped that maybe for a few of us there would be a happy ending.

Here and there, obscured by the trees, we could see tall timber structures, which further along the line were more visible and looked far more sinister. The structures were nothing else than guard towers on four corners of a fenced area. The train was now going very slowly, and finally stopped. In front of us there was only forest, the tracks finished here. Was this it? My heart was full of expectation.

The door was opened and I could see the fence and the towers similar to the ones we had passed, but my mind was elsewhere. I had to find out without delay. There were some people outside and I jumped when, coming closer to them, I could hear my own language. I looked at the faces, but there was no one I recognized. I had to speak to someone. Maybe I should delay before asking, but I could not. "Can you please tell me who is here? Is there a family by the name of Sobierajski. Please tell me they are here." Pause – he says he does not know, he has not been here long. I approached others and asked again, but received the same response – they do not know, they have been here only days. It soon became clear that this place had only recently been occupied, and then by part-families like us.

5

Lesopunkt 5

Our life in cattle trucks came to an end after a fortnight or so of indescribable misery, squalour and the tension of people living in conditions where privacy was non-existent. And yet we had come to know each other and form a kind of bond that would not have been possible in any other circumstances.

The place at the end of the line was called LESOPUNKT 5 and resembled the other four we had passed on our way. It stood in the middle of a clearing, surrounded by woods on all sides and sandwiched between a railway line and a small brook. The main compound was approximately 100 yards square, fenced by vertical half logs ten feet high with the top ends sharpened to points like pencils. Each corner had a high roofed watch tower and there was one double gate on the side facing the railway. Entering through the gate, on the left stood a long administration hut, with the offices of our Commandant, his staff and some soldiers. Right and left of the square were living huts for the inmates. At the rear there were two buildings, one known as *Bania* housing sauna and disinfection room. The sauna room had one corner stacked with rocks and a fire underneath. When the rocks were heated enough water was poured over them giving steam that rapidly filled the room. The other building at the rear was described as an eating hut, never to be forgotten for the red-coloured placard with white letters reading:

LESOPUNKT

"WHO DOES NOT WORK, DOES NOT EAT".

Outside the compound near the railway line stood a roofed shed with no walls, housing a steam engine which drove a circular saw and a small generator. From the railway line, along the left and rear side, ran a small brook with a wooden bridge that lead to some workhouses and stables.

All buildings were made of wood, walls were made of full logs laid horizontally, with moss joints and no cladding to the inside faces. Timber-trussed roofs were covered in wooden shingles. The floor was raised above ground level and consisted of thick timber planks, and in the middle of the floor stood a cast iron heating stove. The living huts were furnished with boarded bunk beds along both sides. The whole place gave an impression of recent construction, as though completed just before our arrival.

The gate was open, unsupervised, and the towers were empty. It puzzled me why so much security was built and not

" WHO DOES NOT WORK, DOES NOT EAT "
LESOPUNKT

used. At the time it did not occur to me, but later I often wondered whether the whole complex was built for other purposes.

Still with my guardian and her daughter, we were led by an unarmed soldier to a hut behind the admin block, on entering which we found some of the bunks already taken. The empty ones were near the door. I was allocated a top layer of boards not far from my companions. I raised my suitcase still wrapped in a quilt, put it at the head of the bunk and climbed up and lay down, confused and unable to understand what had happened to me in such a short time. The month of March, 1940, was coming to an end.

Looking around the hut I saw women and children of all ages. Among them I noticed a boy of similar age to myself and I was pleased to notice he wore a gimnazjum uniform. Shyly he looked at me, gave me a smile exposing two large front teeth, reminding me of a rabbit. The room was full of voices; a lot of information was being exchanged between grown-ups, while us children listened. Comparing the whys, wheres, whens, hows, etc, it became clear to me that the experiences did not vary much. We had all been absent from home that night, then collected and brought here with the same promise. But nobody knew where the rest of their families were. They had all arrived only days ago and more trains were expected since there were still empty huts. Apart from work inside the compound such as cleaning offices, helping around the kitchen and the bania, there was outside work carried out by some women, but chiefly by men. Although we had not seen many men, we were told that there are quite a few who, like us, had not been at home that night. They lived in huts opposite ours and during the day they worked in the forest cutting down trees. Others, using a horse-drawn two-wheel truck, transported the logs to the sawmill, where still others would cut them to the required sizes and load them on to trains to be taken away. This conversation went on and on. Interesting and informative though it was, I felt completely exhausted. All I wanted to do was to fall asleep in this unreal world and wake up free from this nightmare.

The next day all new arrivals were told to collect their clothing, bedding and go to the bania building. There we undressed, passed our belongings to the disinfecting room and stayed behind naked in the room full of steam. After a while our bundles came back with that peculiar smell not easily forgotten or got rid of. Some blankets were distributed and we got dressed and returned to our huts, hoping to be lice-free from now on.

It was not long before I made friends with the rabbit-toothed boy. His name was Tadek and he came from the north-east of Poland and, like myself, was attending a gimnazjum away from home. His uniform was in a worse state than mine and there were holes in his trousers which I thought he should have mended. His bunk was a mess; general untidyness was everywhere around him. For all his obvious shortcomings, he made up for it by a face which always had the suggestion of a smile: it must have been his teeth that made him look so happy, because, later on, in times of sadness, he still had that smiling face. There were other boys like us, he told me, scattered around the different huts: The older boys were working in the forest while the younger ones were employed in part-time work at the saw mill. There were no restrictions on our movements; you could wander outside the compound, the gate being closed only at night, but, since deep snow lay everywhere, walking was confined to well-trodden footpaths.

One by one my wagon companions were required to go to the admin hut. When my turn came I was not unduly concerned, for it seemed that nothing worse could happen. I entered a room where a soldier was sitting behind a desk covered with official looking papers and there was that portrait again. I had to retell my story, including details of my family, and in response to my question "Where are they?" he gave me the standard reply that he did not know, but enquiries would now be made and, when it was established, he would see what could be done. All the information I gave him would be forwarded to the Commandant, he said. Then followed the rules and regulations that I must observe: these were numerous, but the ones I remembered were to report every morning to the admin hut when I would be allocated work if there was any on the day; I must not try to escape. If I did and was caught I would be punished. Although there were no restrictions on our local movements, I must not go far. I would also be issued with meal tickets. After the interview I felt a bit more hopeful. The attitude of the soldier, who was middle-aged and mild-mannered, seemed to show sympathy for the situation I was in.

My newly found friend took me to the eating hut. The room was the same as ours, except that instead of bunk boards there were wooden tables and benches along both long walls, and of course the red placard with white letters and, need I mention, the obligatory picture. Both short walls had a serving hatch, one to the kitchen, the inside of which I never saw. The other led to a shop, but since there was practically nothing to buy, my friend told me, especially in the food line, there was hardly any trade done. Apart from that, you had to have money. We queued for our meals, which was always a soup and some bread. The most common soup was called *shchy,* followed by fish soup. The first was mainly cabbage, sometimes with potatoes, and on rare occasions you could find a bit of meat which later I found out to be horse meat. It was the same with the fish soup; you found a bone now and then but rarely any meat. You received your soup in treasured-by-all tin cans with a wire handle and ate with a wooden spoon. Tadek led me to a table where a number of boys he knew already sat. Among them was a pleasant boy, rather short and podgy with a round face, in a uniform like ours. The three of us became firm friends. We had not failed to notice girls of our own age coming to this hut, and in days to come a visit here became a highlight of our grey exis- tence. Smiles, eye to eye contact at first, progressed into mild flirtation, very innocent and always in groups. The hut became our meeting place. Here we talked, made plans, played games and invented nicknames for each other. Because I still wore a scarf I had brought from Poland I was known as "yellow scarf". Downhearted as we were, we found comfort in being together and sharing our troubles.

Whenever possible, the three of us were together. Each morning we met outside the admin hut waiting for our assign- ments. Most days we were told to go to the sawmill and report for work, which consisted mainly of keeping the place tidy. We swept the floors, collected waste material to be burnt a safe distance away, stored cut logs ready for transport and helped load the trains. We preferred to be near the railway line where there were trains coming and going. We met several wagons bringing more part-families and we could see the disappointed faces when told that their relatives were not here.

Winter was to last another four to five weeks; the weather was still very cold, penetrating our flimsy uniforms, so, as often as we could, we would warm our bodies against the ever-running steam engine. For our labour we were paid very little, but at least we had some income. We stayed together, comfortable in each other's company.

My adopted mother worked in the forest to begin with, but before long she was transferred to the office block as a clerk. I could have been wrong, but I suspected that her charm and beauty contributed to her rapid promotion. As time went by my guardian had less and less concern for me. She stopped asking me how I was and how my day was and what I had been doing. She even stopped nagging me to keep my place tidy. At first I thought that she was probably tired and it would not be long before she was her normal self again, but it never happened. Slowly but surely, although we still spoke to each other, we never recaptured the close relationship we had had before. Probably, and I regret it often, I should have shown her more gratitude, or at least said "thank you" more often for all the motherly care she gave me.

I cannot recall when and how I found out about the post – people were writing letters to Poland. Hastily I wrote a letter to my aunt, but of course it was not to Poland any more; that part belonged to our liberators. I posted the letter with my address, hoping it would reach its destination, but with less hope of receiving a reply.

The days were getting warmer; the snow was going down and winter was nearly over. We spent our time near the sawmill whether we were wanted there or not. At first we thought it was an optical illusion, but in the days to come we were sure that the rails on the line were twisting and sloping in all directions. The trains, though small, travelled slowly and with care. Each time we looked the lines were worse and eventually there were no more trains. As the snow melted away and grass became visible, in places the rails became suspended on stumps of trees, hitherto hidden below the snow. It was amazing to see the rails and sleepers misshapen and distorted, hanging in the air. It was obvious that the line had been built in the winter on top of snow. Immediate arrangements were made to put the matter right. All able bodies were set to work to remove the unwanted stumps, and, where possible, the line was relaid. The bulk of the work was done by men from Lesopunkt 4 as that was the only length of the line affected. In less than a week the railway was back to normal, this time laid on solid ground.

Collecting my ration of soup one day, a woman who worked there who often smiled at me whispered to me to come to the back door after the meal. She opened the door and gave me something wrapped in paper. Before I could say thank you the door was closed. She had been rather secretive about it, so, without showing it to anyone, I opened it in private to find inside a piece of meat. I had not tasted anything as delicious as this for a very long time. I was extremely grateful to her for we were always hungry. I never found out her name, but in a roundabout way I discovered that she had a son somewhere in Russia. Whenever possible, or when she could get away with it, she just nodded her head and I knew that if I went to the back door I would be given something to eat.

For us boys who did not really work because of our age, the red placard meant what it said, just the bare minimum, but for those who worked the food was more plentiful. They had to complete what was known as the norm, but if anyone exceeded the norm he was called a *Stahanovec*. This meant the best food there was, normally pieces of meat or fish, and more bread. In addition, they were paid better and had first choice of goods such as clothing and footwear when these were available in the shop. I was most envious of boots called *Valonki*. They were made out of compressed wool and looked very warm, but, not being one of the privileged and not having the money, I never had a pair.

Spring came suddenly. The sun shone warmly and green colours were everywhere. It was on one of those beautiful mornings that I was selected to go to the stables. I had no idea why and leaving my friends did not please me, but I did not dare to argue. Waving goodbye, I slowly walked towards the bridge over the stream and up a slight incline when I heard noises to my right. I stopped, made a few steps in the direction of the sound, and there through the trees I could see a horse standing motionless and a man with an axe beside the animal. The man raised his axe and with the blunt end hit the horse in the middle of the forehead. The horse shuddered, but was still on his four legs. The man repeated the action and this time the legs gave in and the horse fell. I did not wait to see what happened next, but suspected that the animal had served its purpose and now the kitchen would have its long awaited fresh supply of meat. At the stables I was given three horses, two to be delivered to Lesopunkt 4 and the other one to be my transport there and back. I took note of how to get there and set out on my journey through the corridors of thick forest, for there were no roads, just long clearings which I presumed were precautions in case of fire. Nearing my destination, I saw gangs of men working near the woods, guarded by soldiers with rifles and long bayonets. I found the stables, delivered the horses and had a brief chat with a man there who was Russian. He told me that all the men here were Russian *Zakluchony,* meaning a kind of prisoner, and that they had built Lesopunkt 5 and also relaid the railway.

Often, with my two friends, when we were not at work and the day was sunny, we would go for a walk along the stream. The water was not deep enough for a swim but the sound of the stream and the freshness in the air took me back to my home. At moments like this I felt a lump in my throat and asked God, "When will I be there again?" Gradually we ventured further into the woods where we found some red berries which I recognized as edible. At last we had found something we could eat. What is more, I thought, if there are berries there must be mushrooms, not now but maybe later. I shared my thoughts with my friends and the prospect of finding and eating cooked mushrooms pleased us. One day when I was alone with Tadek we went deeper into the woods where we found a fallen log and sat on it talking. I cannot remember whether it was he or I, but one of us asked what would happen if we started a fire. We started collecting dry wood and moss, and Tadek produced a box of matches bought at the shop. With his ever-present smile he said, "Let's burn the place down." A fire was lit and we ran back as fast as we could. Once inside we watched the sky in the direction from where we came, but there was no smoke. We waited, hardly speaking, but there was nothing. We looked at each other, shrugged our shoulders and parted.

One happy day I received a letter from my aunt and I was overjoyed. There it was, clearly written an address of my family near a town called Kotlas in the Archangel region, which I knew to be far north in Siberia. Oh, thank you God. At least I know they are alive and where they are. Never mind if it is Siberia, never mind how, I will get there. But first I must write a letter to them, which I did immediately. At the time I had no idea of the trauma my parents were going through, not knowing whether their only son was dead or alive. Only now, having children of my own, can I appreciate the terrible suffering they lived through.

More and more letters arrived from our homeland. The main topic of conversation now was the addresses and whether they matched. To my knowledge they never did. They varied greatly, scattered around the vast area of the Union of Soviet Socialist Republics. The only course of action open to us was to inform the Commandant and plead for him, by whatever methods he could, to reunite our families. This was always done through his staff; to see the Commandant himself was almost impossible. I only ever saw him from a distance.

The lice infection never left us and with time it became worse. In the end we resigned ourselves, admitting there was no way we could be rid of them. My hair was full of them. I was so ashamed of it that I wore a hat everywhere I went. Even during meals I kept it on, which was against the way I was brought up and this bothered me. I remember well how during the nights I would run my hand through my hair and collect dozens of them. Using my fingernails, I would kill them and hear the repeated clicking sounds. It was not unusual, when with my friends, for one to say stand still, so that the lice which normally gathered around a collar could be brushed off. There was no shame in it and no one felt embarrassed. In desperation I came upon an idea; one sunny

day on my own I went to the stream, found a secluded place, undressed and put all my clothing under water with rocks on top. I lay on the grass with my hair immersed and settled down for an hour or so thinking that by then the lice will drown. I was wrong; water had no effect on them at all. I dried my clothing in the sun, got dressed and, disappointed, made my way back.

In addition to lice we had to put up with bed bugs, orange-coloured vermin, the size of small peas when bloated with blood. They lived in the cracks of timber walls and roofs, but at night they would come crawling along the roof and, with pinpoint precision, drop on any exposed flesh. Often you felt the impact and, when killed, they gave out a very unpleasant odour.

Early in the spring Tadek and I were assigned to a man whose job it was to go deep into the forest to select and mark suitable trees to be cut down and delivered to the sawmill.

We were there to carry his tools and generally to help any way we could. To go into the depths of the forest you had to take certain precautions. The ends of sleeves and bottoms of trousers had to be tied around with string. Over your head you wore a netting dropped over the shoulders, and preferably you wore gloves. Uncomfortable as this was in the steamy atmosphere of the thick forest, the gear was essential as protection against mosquito bites. They followed you everywhere in unbelievably large clouds. We lit a fire, making as much smoke as possible, and only then were we able to remove the headwear and gloves. I found the work very tiring, with endless walking from sunrise to sunset, mostly in semi-darkness. You never saw the sun, which was hidden by a roof of foliage. I was getting depressed and often, when the others did not see me, I would get down on my knees and pray: God, if you get me out of this hell, I will never ask you for anything else.

Our pay improved slightly and I desperately wanted to buy some clothing. My clothes were getting tatty, my shoes were wearing out and, as for my underwear, the less said the better. Now and then the shop had a delivery of clothing but by the time the *Stahanovec* had bought theirs, and they had the priority, there was nothing left for me. I just had to manage with what I had. Also, now and then some food could be bought. I remember two occasions. Once the shop was supplied with halva, and another time with butter, and in both cases the quantity must have been greater than normal, for I was able to buy some and had a rare feast. Sometimes the shop had what is known in the Russian language as *Kurushka,* a substitute for tobacco made up of finely cut tobacco stems, not leaves. The only way to smoke it was to shape a piece of newspaper into a cone; the *kurushki* were poured into the wide end, then you bent it into what looked like a pipe, held it in your hand and smoked it, just like you would a pipe. Some of my older friends were already smokers and were good at it. I tried a few times but could never succeed without losing most of the *kurushki,* and gave it up in the end.

Miserable as I usually was, there were days of joy, such as the day I received the first letter from my father. I ran back to my bunk and with trembling hands I opened it and began to read. When I finished my heart was bursting with all kinds of emotions. He ended with: "There is nothing I would not do – to be a bird and fly – to bring you here, to be with us."

At about this time, bitten by insects and vermin, I continuously scratched my legs, where a small abscess appeared, then grew much bigger and my leg swelled badly. Apart from the pain, I could hardly walk. My friend was very concerned and, on advice from the women in the hut, he used to bring different preparations which he applied to my leg, but they had no effect. I remembered that my mother used to prick a small abscess with a needle and suggested he do the same, but after a few unsuccessful attempts we gave up. Matters did not improve, and in the end he found a boy with a small knife who made a cut, applied some pressure to release the pus and wrapped my leg in some cloth. I was in terrible pain and lay on my bunk, but gradually I recovered. To this day, however, I have a large scar to remind me of Lesopunkt 5.

Summer was coming to an end and, when not working, we still walked the banks of the stream, but more often we went with our tin cans to the outskirts of the forest looking for mushrooms. My two friends had little knowledge what to look for, and which mushrooms were edible. Knowing something about them, I was able to give them useful hints but none of us had any idea how to cook them. There were no difficulties in finding them; we cleaned them, cut them into manageable sizes, put them in our cans, started a fire, and boiled them for an hour or so. When we thought the mushrooms were ready, we ate them with our wooden spoons, regardless of taste. Enjoyable as our meals were, we often suffered from long periods of diarhhoea. I suspected that it was not the mushrooms we picked but the way we cooked them. For a change, one day we decided to go in a different direction behind the stables. We had walked quite a distance when we came upon a clearing full of what looked like potatoes. Not giving much thought, we rushed forward when

Bang! Bang! We stopped dead in our tracks. Someone was shooting at us. Frightened, we ran back to hide behind the trees. We never found out who was shooting or whether there were any real potatoes, but we never went in that direction again.

My birthday came and went. Autumn was in the air and my visits to the admin hut became more and more frequent. Suddenly one day I was told that a number of people, including myself, would be released to go and join their families. What happiness I felt at that moment. I had to share the good news with my friends and everyone I met, and of course I wrote to my father saying I would shortly be on my way. That night I prayed with gratitude. Before long I learned more details: the names of the group going; there were seven of us; we were to travel on a train to Archangel with a soldier as our guide. From there we would go by steamboat to Kotlas. Here we would be separated for our final destination. I did not know any of my future companions and no one was going to the place I was bound for. The date of my departure was not given, but all being well we should begin our journey at the end of October, 1940.

6

North With Hope

The last day at Lesopunkt 5 I spent packing my belongings, saying goodbye to my friends, promising to keep in touch, then a short walk to the admin block to join the others. The most noticeable member of the group was a middle-aged man who was head and shoulders above the rest, with a thoughtful face. The only other man looked the oldest among us; he was much smaller and kept himself to himself. Standing slightly away from us were two Ukrainian brothers some ten years older than me. How and why they were here I did not ask and they did not tell me. Completing the group was a mother with a child. She was of average height, not very old and had a worried face. Her child was at a sweet and interesting age, just learning to walk. Eventually we were joined by an unarmed oldish soldier and we all walked slowly towards the railway.

We did not need to look back. We would never forget the evil-looking fence and towers. That ugly sight will stay in my memory for ever. After seven months of hopelessness, hunger and misery, we were boarding the train with new hope in our hearts. There was little talk; everything was done almost silently, as though afraid we would wake up to find it was only a dream. We settled down as best we could in a wagon similar that we had travelled in before and began the journey back to Suhobezvodnaya. The scenery did not interest us. We could see in our minds the monotonous expanse of forest and

46

we knew we would be passing four other Lesopunkts on our way. Our minds were preoccupied with what lay ahead. Our soldier guide, though not very talkative, warned us to stay together. He would look after our needs, whatever these might be – food, train connections or anything else – and he would see us safely to Archangel. Most of the questions came from the tall man who, with time, became our leader.

From Suhobezvodnaya we travelled for the first time in a passenger train in comfort I hadn't experienced for some time. We tried to stay together; only when the train was crowded would we be apart. When this happened I would keep a close watch on the others, anxious not to be separated. Long stops were infrequent, mostly at the major stations, and then our guide would go in search of food, in which he was quite successful. Often he would lead us to the station buffet for the customary soup and bread. He must have had his heart in the right place, for on occasions he would come back with something for the baby, such as milk or sweets. Once, I remember, we spent a night at a station and slept on a crowded floor in a waiting room. Not finding enough space, I slept away from the others and was awoken by a man in a military uniform and asked to produce identity papers, which I did not have. He was rather suspicious when I tried to explain where my papers were and led him to our guide to resolve this matter to his satisfaction.

Throughout the journey we never became a close unit. The two brothers were understandably isolated and kept to themselves. The others, being so much older, formed a separate group where most of the discussions and planning took place. I was always last in queues getting on or off the trains and rarely involved in conversation. I felt as if nobody would worry if I disappeared. Not surprising, I became withdrawn and lonely. I wondered whether the Russian experience had made me self-centred and selfish, or was this the rule of survival. The only consolation I could find was turning my thoughts to my family and the warm welcome I hoped soon awaited me.

Snow was beginning to fall when we reached Archangel.

From the station our guide took us to a harbour building with an enormous waiting room full of people. I hated the place the moment we entered. There was no room to move, the air was blue with smoke and, above all, everywhere was the smell of human sweat. As I later found out, there was also an acute shortage of toilets. Our guide deposited our papers in one of the offices, telling us that from now on we must look after ourselves. The office would tell us when and where a steamboat would be available to take us up the River Dvina to Kotlas. After the goodbyes, our guide wished us well and left us. We were sorry to see him go, for his presence had given us a sense of security for the first half of our journey.

Had it been a day or two our waiting would have been bearable, but a week went by and we were still there, beginning to wonder if we would ever leave this depressing place. The tall man now really became our leader. He was the one who went regularly to the office enquiring about our onward transport, always with the same answer: no room at the moment, maybe tomorrow. We had no doubt that our names had the lowest priority and, if we were to succeed in getting a place on a boat, a different approach had to be made. Meanwhile, as days dragged on, food was our top priority. Just off the hall there was a small eating room which was always full, with long queues, regardless of whether the room was open or closed. We seemed to spend our days just queueing, with someone staying behind to guard our belongings and the floor space where we slept. Next time our leader went to the office he took with him the mother and her child, hoping to get a more sympathetic reaction. This move must have worked, because, a few days later, we were given the date and name of the steamboat which would take us on.

Winter comes early to these northern parts of Russia and cold, fresh air greeted us as we walked out of that stinking hall and made our way towards the harbour. Snow was everywhere, making our white-painted boat look even smaller. I found myself once more at the back as we walked down the gangway on to an open part of what I now recognized to be a paddle steamer. Both the front and the rear sections were roofed and had walls, and the rear portion was lined with bed bunks. The front was full of compartments which I did not know the use of, among them was a small kitchen. The middle portion had a funnel in the centre. Though roofed, it had no walls, and around the funnel, shoulder high, logs were stacked vertically.

Soon I realized that we had been the last to embark. All the bunks were occupied and people were sitting on the floor. I went around and came out through the door on the other side, hoping to see the others and confer on our next move. I waited, but no one came. I was on my own once again. Thinking of searching once more, I opened a door, but in front of me all I could see were hostile looks from a room full of strangers. Desperate, I retraced my steps and sat down on my suitcase, a very lonely boy. Nobody came to talk to me, nobody cared. Could there have been a more unwanted boy in the whole wide world I wondered, as tears rolled down my cheeks.

As soon as the boat moved away I knew that if I were not to freeze, I had to find some shelter. Having no walls, this portion of the boat became unbearably cold. Looking around, the logs caught my eyes and an idea came to my mind. I got up and began to rearrange the logs to form a recess. It occurred to me that, if I made it deep enough, I would have the benefit of the heat from the funnel. Carefully I constructed a kind of corridor a few metres long, laid my suitcase at the end, wrapped myself in the quilt and sat down. I was very satisfied with my efforts. I could feel the heat and the logs around and above me cut down the draught. I was sure I would survive. What I did not know was that the boiler burnt a vast quantity of wood. Soon a floor hatch opened and a man came out. He saw me and we stared at each other, he in disbelief, myself very frightened of what he would say. If I couldn't stay here, what would I do, where would I go? A faint smile came over his face and I felt safer. I got up and walked towards him. After I had explained my predicament and offered to help carry the logs to the hole in the floor he

STEAMBOAT - RIVER DVINA

nodded in agreement. As time went by the logs were disappearing rapidly, but we managed to keep my nook undisturbed, and when we stopped to replenish the wood he allowed me to stay there.

I never saw any documents that permitted us to travel by train or on this boat. These had been in the possession of the soldier before, and were now with our leader. They must have entitled us to free passage and food, however meagre it was, for I had not paid for anything, except in the shops, and this was rare, as I had little money and the shops, when available, had little of what I wanted, which was always food. Although there were not many people moving about in my portion of the boat, I knew that sooner or later I would meet up with the rest of the group. Kitchen queues were being formed when I saw them. They found my hole in the logs, but I thought I was better off there than in the overcrowded floor space they occupied. We stood in the queue together

50

and, on the strength of the documents our leader produced, we were given our ration of food.

The enormously wide mouth of the river gradually narrowed and occasional ice flows drifted past. The banks on both side, and as far as the eye could see, were covered in snow, making our progress seem slow. The scenery, as I watched it in the short hours of daylight, seemed serene and peaceful, disturbed only by the sound of the paddle steamer. I watched until well into the night, and it helped me to forget my hole in the logs. Eventually I retired and, with my quilt wrapped around me, I sat down and fell asleep.

A few days into the journey the weather worsened. Snow was falling heavily and ice flows increased considerably in size and number. The speed of the boat had been reduced by continuous collisions with the ice and by manoeuvres to avoid it. The boat's captain must have realized the struggle ahead as conditions deteriorated. In the distance we could see a small landing platform on the west bank and it became obvious that the boat was aiming in that direction. With some difficulty we docked against the platform and stopped. We had not even completed half the journey. Despair could be seen on all our faces. What would happen now?

Before long the Russian passengers, and there were many of them, disembarked, leaving our group behind with night approaching. This at least offered me the chance of a bunk and I was looking forward to a good rest when a horse sledge drew alongside. We were told to load our belongings and to follow the sledge, which had just enough room to accommodate the mother and her child.

As we walked in the dark through this bitterly cold night each step made a peculiar squeaking sound which became familiar to me later; it only occurs in really freezing conditions. We had not gone more than a couple of miles when we came upon a built-up area and stopped in front of a long one-storey brick building. There, waiting for us, was a man who, after a short conversation with our leader, led us to a long corridor inside. Pointing to the two brothers and myself, he opened the first door on his left indicating our accommodation. By the time I entered the small room with three iron beds, the brothers were already putting their luggage on the beds against the end wall, leaving me with a bed nearest the door. Nobody said much. We were tired, made ourselves as comfortable as possible on the straw-filled mattresses and went to sleep.

Raipromcombinat was the name of the place, which meant Regional Industrial Estate, with a fair number of warehouses and one brick kiln. It was situated not far from a sizeable village called, if my memory served me right, Vinogradov. In the morning, after an early meal in the canteen, we were allocated to different works. I was told to report to the brickyard which was the largest enterprise on the estate. The works consisted of a huge shed where bricks were made, then delivered to the kiln nearby for firing. Without any skills in that field, I was given a wheelbarrow to transport the newly made bricks to the kiln and, when ready, to remove them to a storing place. From day one I knew I could not manage the job given me. I had to work outside, pushing the loaded wheelbarrow to and fro in freezing weather. My clothing, still the same in which I had left Poland, offered no protection at all against the cold. My shoes, practically worn out, were completely unsuitable for snow, yet I carried on. A few weeks on and I was in a dreadful state. My hands, toes and knees were frostbitten and I was getting weaker, hardly able to push the wheelbarrow. The man in charge noticed my sorry condition, told me to go to my room and wait until alternative employment could be found.

My next job was a lot easier. I was to help in the warehouse where baskets were being made out of willow twigs. The room was not very big, full of tables and stools where only women and older men worked. Here I met a chargeman who was an Ukrainian deported by Stalin in the purges of 1930. He was rather thick-set, in his forties and with a large moustache, giving him the appearance of a cold, hard man, but he was exactly the opposite. He must have liked me, or felt sorry for me, for I was given the easiest of tasks, preparing

VINOGRADOV

the twigs, distributing them around the room and keeping the fire going. When possible he taught me basket-weaving.

Unknown to me at the time, our leader had not given up hope of our continuing our journey, and often pressed the management to let us proceed on our way. I was sure that we would stay until the end of winter. Come spring, the boat would be able to reach Kotlas as previously planned.

My lice problem had not gone away. I still wore my hat at all times and my room companions could not help but notice my plight. The only way to deal with the infested hair, I was told, was to wash it in Kerosene, but where and how to get it they did not know. At the first opportunity, I mentioned this to my chargehand and not long after he produced a bottle. Further, I was advised to go to the bania, (every place in Russia seemed to have one) take off my clothes, put them at the highest level in the room and stay there for an hour or so, at the same time washing my hair in Kerosene. I followed this advice and, to my surprise and delight, it proved to be successful, except that my hair had a white, speckled look.

These were the eggs which you could not remove. So one of my roommates gave me a short back and sides; only then could I remove my hat without feeling ashamed.

Christmas, 1940, was approaching and for the first time in my short life I was not looking forward to it. I had prayed from the outset of my journey north that my reunion with my family might coincide with Christmas and had imagined the happiness of being among them. But how can you celebrate when you are lost somewhere in Siberia and you are alone?

In communist Russia there is no Christmas, no holiday. You work normally. This, I thought, would help me to overcome my emotions when the time came. I did not see preparations by any of my companions, and I was glad that, like myself, they too probably wanted to forget Christmas this year. Days being so short, it was dark when you left and came back from work and so it was on Christmas Eve. I came back to an empty room, but, try as I did, I could not dismiss from my mind the significance of the evening. I wanted to hide from myself and from the thoughts of my family somewhere praying that I was well and still on my way. I could not restrain my emotions any longer. I lay on my bed, pulled the quilt over my head and wept uncontrollably.

My despair was interrupted by the brothers returning from work. Seeing the miserable state I was in, they told me that they had a surprise for me. I watched them as they produced the ingredients and prepared a *kutia* on our stove. This apparently is a typical Ukrainian Christmas Eve dish. In our difficult situation, it was only a sweetened boiled wheat grain, whereas normally dried fruit and spices are added. We did our best to look and sound cheerful, while we shared the *kutia,* but it was only skin deep. Presently the rest of the group came in and we wished each other well, but most of all for a speedy reunion. Sitting on the beds, we quietly sang a few carols and our leader informed us that his persistence had been sympathetically received. It should not be long before we were on our way. He had no knowledge of the type of transportation but had expressed his willingness to take whatever transport was given and asked us how we felt about it. No one argued, as we were all anxious to go, but we voiced some reservations, mainly concerning the severity of the winter. In the end we agreed to wait for more details, when the final decision would be taken.

On one of my days off I made up my mind to go and see the village. The weather was reasonable, rather cold with crisp snow under foot and the sun shining. I followed the tracks of sledges and lorries, these being the only visible signs of the road. After a couple of miles I came upon a valley. On one side was the village in the distance, and on the other side there were some buildings and what looked like a windsock. I walked a bit faster to have a better view, and sure enough there was a small aeroplane. I stopped for a while gazing at the machine, which I had never expected in this wilderness. I imagined how easy it would be to complete my journey if only . . .

I waited some time to see if the plane would take off, but in vain. There was no movement on the other side of the valley. Disappointed, I turned and continued on my way and before long I was on the outskirts of the village. The houses were mostly one-storey buildings with roofs completely covered in thick snow. Only the smoking chimneys were visible. Walls, where exposed, were of timber construction, some cladded in boards, others had horizontal logs. Practically all the houses were narrow rectangles, the shorter sides facing the main road, having two windows with decorative surrounds. Along one long side ran a footpath now dug out in snow, which led to an entrance somewhere in the middle. I could not see many people about as I walked the length of the main street. Then I came to a two-storey brick building with big letters proclaiming it to be a "Palace of Culture" where I could see groups of youngsters. I remember standing there, shy and undecided whether to go in or not, but finally I forced myself up the stairs and opened the door. The room I entered was a main hall, very warm, with table tennis stands and tables with chess boards, all of them being used by young girls and boys. Hesitatingly, I moved forward, very aware of strange looks in my direction, and sat down on one of the benches along the wall. I did not intend to stay long, just enough to satisfy my curiosity, and, if possible, to buy something to eat. I looked around and saw a doorway where youngsters went in and out. Gathering enough courage I followed them to find it was a cinema. In a dim light I found a seat near the front and, feeling warm and secure in the darkness, I sat down to watch the show. During an interval I again followed the crowd, this time to a canteen where I was able to buy a glass of chicory tea and a kind of bread cake. By now nobody paid particular attention to me. Feeling more at ease I went back to the cinema to watch another film about the war with Japan. One scene particularly stuck in my mind, of a well-camouflaged Russian soldier lying on the ground, who got up now and then to kill a Japanese soldier. When the show was over I walked out into the night, glad I made the effort, and returned to Raipromcombinat.

The basket-making warehouse was running short of willow twigs and my Ukranian chargehand wanted me to go with him to fetch a new supply. We would be away two days and spend the night in a cabin there. There was no need to worry, he announced. He made this trip regularly and would take care of me. We left early in the morning with a horse-drawn sledge. At first we were on well-defined roads, but soon we were in virgin snow with no tracks to follow. He assured me he knew the way and eventually we arrived at what was a frozen lake, with plenty of willow twigs projecting through the ice. He insisted we load up the sledge without delay, to have it ready in the morning, for we would be taking a different route on our return. We worked in slushy snow and by the time the load was ready I was damp throughout, especially my feet. He found the small cabin easily: it had bunk beds on each side and a narrow passage in the centre but no heating. On our way to the cabin we collected some dry wood and my companion started a fire. Out of a sack he pulled some bread and dried fish which we held on a stick against the fire and had a reasonable meal, followed by a hot drink, using the essential tin can, in which

the snow was melted and boiled. By now the darkness was all around us.

What happened next I was to regret later and even now when I think about it, and I often do, shivers run down my spine. My companion took off his wet boots and socks and dried them near the fire, suggesting I should do the same. Whether I was too tired or too lazy, or for other reasons I do not remember, I did not take his advice. With some blankets which he gave me I left him and climbed on one of the bunks. I covered myself the best I could, hoping for a night's rest and sleep. The temperature must have dropped for I suddenly woke up shaking with cold and my feet freezing. I was scared, afraid that if I fell asleep I would not wake up. I did not want to disturb my friend. Anyway, what could he do if I woke him up? I kept moving my toes and turning from side to side. To say I had an uncomfortable night is less than the truth, and morning could not have come too early. He got up before me and started a fire outside. I joined him, pretending all was well, never admitting how foolish I had been. We had a hot drink, warmed ourselves for a while and left the little cabin somewhere in Siberia.

There was no room to sit on the sledge so we walked behind. To begin with I found I could not keep up, but slowly life came back to my feet. We set out on a different route and soon came to a road which led us to a small village. My friend knew his way around and before long we entered a room at the back of a house where lots of people were sitting at tables having meals. He knew some of them and greeted them warmly, especially a woman behind a small counter, who later brought two bowls of hot fish soup with some bread. For the first time I found a chunk of fish, greatly appreciated. We rested a while in a warm room, then got up, said our goodbyes and went on our way. Throughout our journey we talked a lot, he about the Ukraine, I about Poland. Neither of us could find the words to express the hate we felt for *Batcko* Stalin as he was called – *Batcko* means father. He also told me (and this I did not know) about millions of Ukrainians who had been deported from their fertile lands to all parts of Siberia and who now had settled down and built new homes. It was almost dark when we got back to Raipromcombinat.

February was over when the leader informed us of arrangements being made for us to leave in a few days. There was no choice, we all had to go. We would not be going to Kotlas as originally planned but to the nearest railway station, from where we were to leave for our separate destinations. We would have a sledge with a horse for our luggage, maybe with enough room for a mother and a child. The rest of us would have to walk. We would be travelling from village to village where we would stay each night, also to change transport and all being well we should be there in a week or so.

Reactions were predictable. We were all happy to resume our interrupted journey, but the prospect of a long walk alarmed some of us, including myself. My main worry was my shoes, which, after the trip to the lake, had practically disintegrated. When wrapped in rags for warmth they were too small for my feet. This precaution was essential in the middle of a Siberian winter, considering that the temperature could drop as low as minus 50°C. I mentioned my problem to my roommates who agreed that I could not last the distance in the shoes I had, and, after a short discussion, they came up with a proposition. They had a spare pair of shoes much larger than mine, which, if repaired, could just see me through. They also noticed that in my suitcase I had a small leather briefcase used for carrying books when I was at school. If I gave them the briefcase they could use the leather to repair not only the pair they were to give me, but also repair their own. I was pleased with the outcome. Although the 'new' pair were well worn, they looked much better than mine. Now I had to find some pieces of cloth for my feet. I spoke to my moustached Ukrainian friend about the forthcoming journey and my footwear, and not long after produced some rags, for which I was very grateful.

On the morning of our departure the sledge showed up, driven by a local man who said he would take us to the next village, from where another sledge would be provided and he would return home. We loaded up our belongings on that frosty day and set out. This part of Russia is not densely populated, mostly covered by vast expanses of woodland. Villages are far apart and connected by roads cut in the forest, with little traffic and hardly visible, recognized only by a local man. We soon learned to use the tracks made by the sledge and followed each other in single file, myself at the rear. We rarely stopped and if for any reason someone was left behind catching up at early stages of our journey was easy. Later it became more difficult. None of us had anything like the clothing necessary for this bitter climate. To stop my nose freezing inside I covered my nose and mouth with my yellow scarf, and breathed through it. To be on the move, and in our case walking, was not a drawback but the only way to keep your body warm and your feet from freezing. Beating your arms around your shoulders was a common sight. Once a village was reached, very often at night, our sledge driver would deliver us to the local police station. From there we were distributed in twos and threes to different houses.

Until then I had not been inside a Russian home or met a

Russian family. My contact had been limited to men in authority, mostly wearing military uniforms. I had nothing but contempt for communism and its people for the wrongs done to me, my family and millions of Poles. I expected all Russians to be my enemies, to hate me for no other reason than my nationality and my religion, I could not have been more mistaken. The families I met were not communists and most of them did not want to know the meaning of it, not because they were backward people, but because their hard life left no room for abstract ideals. They were hard-working, but had very little to show for their labours. What they had they shared with me, maybe more so when I told them how I came to be among them.

We were always welcomed in the front room, where we would sit with them around the table for a meal. The food was simple: on most occasions it consisted of boiled potatoes, eaten with pickled mushrooms or cucumbers and a hot drink after. If you looked around the room you would see a small curtain in one corner. Hidden behind it would be an icon, beautifully framed and surrounded by family heirlooms, with a lighted candle in front. Heating was provided by a *"piechka"*. This was a large brick oven reaching to a few feet short of the ceiling. The flat top was wide and long enough for at least one couple to sleep there. The fire opening was a yard or so from the floor level, where family cooking and baking was done. We slept on the floor, covered with straw which formed a communal bed for our small group. At night we spread our wet clothing, foot rags and shoes around the *piechka* to dry and be ready for our morning departure.

Days did not differ greatly, except for the distances between villages. We were making reasonable progress in the freezing weather. Only a few more days and we would reach the railway. Then what I feared most happened. The soles of my shoes parted from the leather tops. This was a major set-back. I had to prevent the snow getting inside, otherwise my feet would freeze. With whatever rags I had I wrapped not only my feet but also the outside of my shoes, then tied them with string. This method, though only partially successful,

made my feet large and heavy, and walking became difficult and laborious. On occasions I had to stop to carry out repairs to my improvised footwear. This was not easy; working with freezing hands on frozen rags and string. Catching up afterwards was beyond my strength and from then on I lagged behind. I was very glad when someone dropped back to keep me company.

Soon worse happened. Apart from getting weaker, I was sure my temperature was rising. I kept this to myself, reasoning that when we reached the railway my troubles would be over. About this time one morning we woke up to a raging snowstorm outside. The sledge did not turn up and we spent the day inside our quarters. I was very glad to have a rest, hoping to wake up the next morning feeling better. The couple we stayed with were past middle age with memories of Russia before the October Revolution. We talked about our immediate past with which they sympathized. They recalled with pleasure the good old days. Towards evening the woman of the house, noticing I was unwell, offered me a small glass of vodka. Although I disliked the smell and taste, I drank it. My head felt much lighter and I retired for the night.

Next morning I woke up feeling much worse. My temperature had not gone away and I felt weak and lazy. I simply did not want to get up, but the fear of being left behind got me to my feet. I got dressed and wrapped my feet as best I could. Before we parted the woman gave me a small bottle filled with *"Samogonka",* which was a home-made vodka. Walking now became an all-out effort, but to help matters I took the occasional sip from the bottle. My steps by now were slow and deliberate as I dragged myself onwards, determined to stay with the others. I was hardly aware that this was the last day of our Siberian walk. I closed my mind to everything around me except the thought of survival and getting there; nothing else mattered. Even when I overheard that a child was not with us on the last leg of our travels I did not want to know. Half-conscious and past caring, I struggled on to the small railway station. I was too ill to care where I was going. My next recollection was of sitting opposite the two brothers on the train. They seemed to be talking and looking in my direction. My eyes were closing; I was asleep again.

How I got there I could not remember, but there I was standing in front of some strange buildings, with no idea where to go. I selected the nearest hut and entered a long corridor with lots of doors on my right. I had no wish to go any further. There was no need to search for my family. I was convinced they were not there. Vaguely, I remembered thinking, "Why am I going to sleep in the daytime and in a corridor?" " But why not?" came the answer: all will be well after you have had a rest. I took a few steps inside, put down my suitcase, removed my quilt, spread it on the floor and lay on it in peace. Then deep sleep overcame me.

"What a pity! Such a nice young boy," and "I wonder where his parents are." Somewhere in the distance I could hear these words spoken in my own language. I listened. The voices were still there when I opened my eyes. I could see a window

where two women were sitting. I was lying on the table near the door. Seeing that I was awake one of the women came over to me, while the other went out and returned with a plateful of hot soup. Patiently they forced me to eat. Exhausted by this effort I went to sleep again.

For a number of days I slept, only to wake up for meals. My recovery was slow, but I had many visitors who all seemed pleased to see me getting stronger. The family who took care of me were deported from Poland on 10 February, 1940, like all the others now living in this internment camp. They came from a small village near Brody, a town in the southern part of my country, where the father was a forester. They had two children, a boy and a girl younger than myself. The room they occupied had a timber platform on one side as a communal bed. The rest of the space was taken up by a cast iron heating stove against an outside wall, and a table near the door.

The mother told me she had been the first to see me lying unconscious in the corridor. She called on neighbouring rooms and soon there was a crowd of women and children gathered around me. All agreed they could not let me die alone in this hostile land. Men were not at hand, they were away working, so the mother and the others carried me to her room. They laid me on a table, removed my wet clothing and shoes and covered me with whatever they could spare. Since there were no medical facilities, they were doubtful whether I would survive the night. Apart from keeping me warm and comfortable, there was not much more they could do. Nevertheless, arrangements were made to keep vigil by my side. For two days I lay restless and running a high temperature which in their opinion were symptoms of pneumonia. Whatever illness I had, I connected it with the dreadful night I spent in the cabin by the frozen lake.

The care shown to me by the family and others was overwhelming. My clothing and shoes were taken away and brought back cleaned and repaired. I had more than enough food, often using their last supplies from Poland. I was continuously invited to visit other families in the hut and share with them my experiences. Boys and girls of my age took me to the eating hut, where young people gathered to recall the happy days of youth, reminding me of Lesopunkt 5. There I found out that they were required to attend a school with Soviet teachers. All of them treated it as a joke, especially when attempts were made to convert them into *"Komsomols"* – young communists. The jokes were mostly concerned with portraits of Stalin which were hung on all classroom walls.

February was nearly over when I felt strong enough to continue what seemed like never-ending travels. I mentioned this and was told that my presence was known to the local administration and I was to report to them as soon as I was well. My young friends took me to the commandant's offices, where I answered lots of questions: how I got here, where I was going. My memories of how I got here were very vague, except for the recollections of the Ukrainian brothers, which seemed to clear the matter. I had no desire to ask about them. I did not want to know why I had been abandoned and I never saw them again. Before I left I was promised transport to Kotlas on the next post office sledge.

A small crowd assembled on the day of my departure and accompanied me to the admin hut. Saying goodbye to the families who saved my life was very emotional. How could I adequately express the feelings of gratitude? Whatever I said I knew would fall short of what was in my heart. After special kisses and thank you to the mother of the family and promises to write, I climbed on the sledge and waved my last goodbyes.

The last stages of my journey north are not very clear. The roads could have been the same I had seen before, just narrow clearings in the woodland, all covered in snow. My companion was a Russian, who made the trip to Kotlas regularly. We stayed a night in one small village, and at night the next day we reached Kotlas. There I remember spending two nights at a local police station. I was given a small room on the first floor, which was a kind of a store full of broken chairs and tables. The window overlooked what seemed to be large harbour buildings. The room was not locked, but I was told to stay there until transport would be available to take me to Vitunino, where my family was.

Very early in the morning I was woken up and told to wait for a sledge which would be picking me up shortly. As before, it was a post office sledge driven by a Russian. He told me we would make one stop during the day, then travel by night and in the morning we would reach our destination. I asked him many questions, but to the most important one his answer was negative. He did not know where my family was. Immediately I dismissed all doubts from my mind. Instead, I began to imagine what awaited me at the end of my twelve months' travels. Where will I see them? What house? What room? Had they moved? What will they do when they see me? These thoughts kept me occupied for the rest of the journey. Only hours were now left and, still in darkness, we crossed a bridge and I could see lights on the other side. It was between 7 and 8 o'clock in the morning when we stopped at the bottom of a hill and my Russian companion told me this was it – now only minutes away. My heart would surely burst if I did not find out soon. I got off the sledge and collected my belongings. There were some people moving about. I ran towards them: "Tell me please, is the Sobierajski family here?" "Yes!" I was told to go up the hill, along the top, then to go down and it was the first hut. I climbed the hill, passing some huts that threw pools of light through the windows. Now down the hill; there was the hut. I rushed forward. I slipped and fell into the snow, I got up and brushed the snow off, a few more steps and I opened the door. There was a long corridor in front of me with doors on both sides. Which door was it? Someone had told me. Yes, I remember, it was the first door on my right. I steadied myself. For a split second this reminded me of a similar situation a year ago, standing in front of the door of my house in Poland. But, no, this was different; they were here. I opened the door of the room. I walked in and stood there. The room was full of familiar faces, I looked closer and there on my right I could see them: My mother sitting on a bed platform with my two younger sisters, and on their left I could see my father and my older sister getting dressed. I was standing only yards away but no one saw me. I could not move; I felt tears on my face; I knew I must speak. I had been away so long, travelled so far; Here I am look at me, but no voice came. How long until someone . . .

My younger sister, Joanna, shouted my name, the unreal nightmarish scene was over. All eyes turned in disbelief. Sobbing uncontrollably, I lunged forward into the open arms of my mother and father. We stood there close together, my parents crying as only parents can when their lost son is found. My two sisters, Lutka and Jaska, as I called them, joined us to share the moment of reunion. One person was missing. She was sitting where my mother had left her. My youngest sister Jagoda was barely three years old when I had last seen her. She hardly remembered me. Shyly she came to us to complete the family. At last we were together! The

emotions I felt then reached such depths that even today the thought of it moves me to tears.

The familiar faces I saw were two more families who occupied the same room, both from Chylin, our hamlet in Poland. One family were our neighbours with their three children who lived just across the road. The other family kept a school in Chylin, also with three children. Happily I went to greet them.

The room began to empty. After all, this was a normal working day. But not for our family; this was the day to celebrate our reunion, also to heal the wounds inflicted on us during the last twelve months. Words did not come easily. For some time holding hands or being in each others' arms was comforting enough and somehow necessary. Our eyes met and, if there was a tear, the joy seemed more genuine and deeper. My mother would not let me go, keeping me close by her side, continuously praising God for my safe return and for answering her prayers. Father's eyes never left me. I must have looked a sorry sight for he kept repeating, "My son, my son, how did you manage to survive?", and why had I not written to them. The last letter they had had from me was from Lesopunkt telling them I was on my way to join them. They feared the worst and suffered greatly each day when their thoughts turned to me, imagining me in all kinds of situations. I felt very guilty for causing them so much additional pain. My sisters could not show me enough affection, especially Joanna who was so proud of noticing me first when I stood there in the doorway. They all thought I was one of the friends waiting for the others to go to work.

We all wanted to talk, but who would begin and where? But before all that my mother, as all mothers will, interrupted the eager questions saying that I must be hungry and left to prepare a meal. Meantime, my father looked again at my clothing and footwear and kept shaking his head in disbelief. I still wore my gimnazjum uniform and coat, which was falling apart, but my footwear brought him to tears again. He began to untie the ropes and rags, then shoes and more rags with amazement at my improvisation. Before long I was stripped of all my clothing and for the time being my father offered me some of his to wear. I was glad nobody mentioned my hair which still had white speckles as a reminder of my lice infestation. Only my mother, when she came with the food, put her hand on my head and I knew she knew what the white specks were.

I enjoyed my mother's cooking, more so when I was told that the meal was of food brought from Poland and purposely kept for my homecoming. I finished with bread and honey and then we settled down on the bed platform and I began to tell them what had happened to me since the last time I had seen them which was Christmas, 1939. Needless to say, there were many emotional moments and more tears, especially when I told them how I was found unconscious in the corridor. Here I described the family and how good they were and also the promise I had made to write to them. My father took the address and not long after wrote to them expressing our family's gratitude for saving the life of a lost boy.

For hours we sat there talking. After my story was told, I
heard for the first time what had happened to them, starting
with the events of that night in February, 1940, very nearly a
year ago.

7

10 February, 1940

To understand and to feel a fraction of the trauma of that night let the family be yours and the time now. The family has retired for night, all is quiet, everyone is asleep. In the darkness and out of nowhere there comes an impatient banging at your doors and windows. The parents wake up in fright, look at each other, then at the clock. It is 4 o'clock in the morning. Father gets up, walks to the door, opens it to be confronted by three men, one with a shotgun pointed at him. He is pushed into the living room, ordered to sit down on the sofa and told to stay there whatever happens; if he disobeys he will be shot. The strangers rush through the bedroom shouting for everyone to wake up and assemble in the living room. Mother enters the room with her children clinging to her, some of them already in tears.

You have three hours to pack and get dressed, you are told, then you will be taken away. Outside there are two sledges, one for your belongings, the other for your transportation. You may take some of your possessions, but no more than a sledge can take. All is to be done quietly and with no questions, and no help from your father; he must not move. What to take? Where to begin? What about the children? Mother has no time for tears; she now knows all depends on her. She leads the two small girls into the kitchen and, with an older girl, begins to collect bedding and clothing from adjoining rooms. Next they go to the attic and bring down sacks of oats and flour. They must not forget the frozen meat, honey, bread, and what about this or that? Time is running out and there are so many things to do. We should be loading up the sledge. Father sits there helpless and heartbroken. In his mind he sees the eighteen years of labour vanishing, soon to be abandoned for ever.

Exhausted by physical effort and mental strain, my mother now thinks of how to feed the family. It must be something fast and nutritious. What else but scrambled eggs? Now are the children warmly dressed? Where are the shoes, hats, gloves? Lastly she must dress herself and find winter clothing for her husband.

The time allocated is nearly over but the hours of terror have not ended yet. Before leaving, the family is subjected to the last deliberate act of cruelty. All personal possessions left behind – books, documents, pictures, family photographs – are vandalized by the night raiders and thrown out into the snow. Apart from the heavy furniture the rooms are bare, with no visible trace of the family that lived there.

No more time, only quick glances through the tears, and the family is outside in the early morning light. Farm animals woken up by the opening and closing of doors begin to make noises anticipating their morning feed. But there are some other noises. Somewhere you can hear horses and the sound of moving sledges but you cannot see them clearly. They come closer, and now you can see six sledges, but your eyes are opening wider. You are staring at a dozen Russian soldiers on horses with rifles and long thin bayonets. The leading soldier comes closer, waving his arms and shouting impatiently in his language for our two sledges to move out.

Mother and children are already sitting on the sledge, one of them holding a small black statue of a horse she picked up on her way out. But not father; he is to walk behind, still threatened with a shotgun. He is glad to be on his own; men do not cry and yet he must or his heart will break. He looks at the familiar farmyard and its buildings, which he helped to build and lets out a cry of pain. Mother hears it, looks back in anguish and pulls her children closer together, but remains calm.

The soldiers on horses take over the escort duty, shouting and urging the convoy to move faster. Father knows that shortly they will be passing his sister's house and he must let them know what happened. He indicates his intention to a soldier, and in response the soldier lowers his rifle; there is no mistaking his refusal. In desperation, he shouts; mother looks back and understands the situation. She gets off the sledge and moves in the direction of the house. A soldier sees her; with shouts and threats he bars her way, but mother, determined, takes a few more steps. The soldier turns his horse on her, snatches her handbag and kicks her hard with his heavy boot. Mother falls, but gets up quickly and runs on. She knocks on the door. The convoy moves on as she knocks again. The door opens. There is no time for conversation. Quickly she tells them what has happened and runs back to rejoin her family.

February in Poland can be the coldest month of the year and so it was on that fateful night. The frost was visible all around, the trees were covered with icicles. The sounds of horses and sledges on the frozen snow breaks the stillness of the morning, with occasional shouts from the soldiers. The convoy is making its way south, towards a village called Biala on Horyn.

More sledges come, and in the improving light it is becoming obvious that the whole hamlet has suffered the same fate. The families, though forbidden to shout, wave at each other. All ten original settlers, with their children under 16 years old, are here and all on the move to unknown destinations and uncertain futures. What thoughts and what sorrows the parents experience when the last of their homes disappear from the horizon. Not one of them will live to see it again. But live they must if only for the sake of the children. The convoy moves silently without stopping until they reach the railway station.

There they see hundreds of similar sledges loaded with people, alongside a row of cattle tracks, with hundreds of

Russian soldiers surrounding them. To hear the shouts and cries of despair from men, women and children being pushed, kicked and hit with rifles, some with bloody faces, is enough to make your pent-up feelings explode. There is no escape; you await your turn with resignation and in a daze your family walks up the wooden ramp into the open door of a cattle truck. With a bang the door closes behind you and you are on your way to Siberia.

8

Vitunino

Vitunino was an internment camp, not of recent construction, built deep in the Siberian forest on the banks of the River Viled. Unlike the concentration camp I had been in, Vitunino had no security fences or watch towers. Both banks rose steeply from the river which was crossed by a wooden bridge. One side of the river was used for timber storage in winter. On the other side were the inmates' huts, built at a high level but overflowing on to lower grounds at each end. Huts near the bridge contained administration offices and living quarters for the Russian staff and their families. Further along the river, and some distance from the huts, were stables and sheds for various stores.

All the buildings were made of wood. They had timber-framed walls, faced on both sides with boards. Roofs were mostly covered with corrugated sheeting, some had wooden shingles, all floors had timber boarding. Each hut was divided into rooms with a long central corridor. Rooms were approximately 20 foot square, and the wall opposite the door had a raised timber platform on which two families slept. Another platform along one of the side walls was occupied by a third family. The other side wall had a *piechka;* as in Russian houses this was a heating and cooking oven. Such possessions as the families had were stored underneath the platform or hung on the walls. Our room housed six grown-ups and nine children: here they lived and slept with hardly room to

74

move and with no privacy at all. The only separation between families were blankets suspended from the ceiling. This over-crowding led to tensions and misunderstandings and often previously friendly families now hardly spoke to each other.

Vitunino had a population of around 1,200 Polish men, women and children. Among them were all but one family from my hamlet in Poland. All my friends, except for Jerzyk, my best friend, were here. He, like myself, was away at high school on that day and never joined his family. What happened to him no one knew and I never saw him again. How times had changed since those days when we played games, went fishing, swimming and skating and behaved like children everywhere. Here, as though in a different time and world, we suddenly grew up; we even talked and walked like men and in many cases the children became the bread-winners.

Other families came from various parts of Poland and

various walks of life. There were teachers, lawyers, policemen, landowners, shop keepers, civil servants, a complete cross-section of Polish society. No less than a million men, women and children were forcibly deported from their homes and all on the same night.

The initial shock suffered by my family, and others, though never forgotten or forgiven, had mellowed somewhat by the time I joined them. No matter how bad the circumstances they had to adapt, and to survive they had to work. My mother, with other women, worked as decorators, painting the inside and outside of the huts. My father, with my 16-year-old sister, formed part of a gang felling trees in the forests. The trees then had their branches removed and the logs were cut to specified sizes ready for transportation. The gang consisted of six or so persons. They depended on each other to carry out the norm. This meant working each day, no matter what weather, even in temperatures of 50°C below zero, after

76

digging channels in deep snow to reach the selected trees. Here, as in Lesopunkt, the same communist dogma applied: "If you do not work, you do not eat." Joanna, my 12-year-old sister, attended a school where only Russian was spoken. Special emphasis was put on learning patriotic Russian songs, which I suspected was a cunning attempt to convert young minds to communist ideology. When not at school she helped mother, or stood in queues for what little was available. My youngest sister, four-year-old Jagoda, was still the baby of the family, not aware of the hardships we were going through, and no memories to haunt her later.

My arrival in the camp soon became news. I was the only newcomer they had had for over a year. My mother was very concerned about my appearance and thought I should have something new to wear but before that I was told to go to the bania. With one of my friends, I walked down a snow-covered slippery footpath to a log cabin near the river. The bania was already in use, full of steam and naked bodies. I was amazed to see some of them walking out to roll in the snow and then return to the hot room. We were not brave enough to venture outside and after a while made our way back. My mother looked at my hair and attempted to remove dead lice eggs still stuck to my hair with a comb, but was only partially successful. My old clothing was thrown away and I was given my father's army outfit. I was especially proud to wear his green army overcoat and his pair of high army boots. My new look met with general approval and my sisters thought I looked rather smart.

I knew I had to go to the administration hut to report my presence and be allocated a job. I was glad my father went instead, for on his return he told me I was to be given a few days' rest, which I needed. There was very little I could do during the short hours of daylight as most of my family and friends were at work. Only when my sister Joanna came back from school had I company to go out with and familiarize myself with my new surroundings. She went everywhere with me, pleased to show off her long-lost brother. Many times we were stopped by people curious to know how a boy of my age had managed to survive such a long journey. I was even allowed to jump queues to get our family provisions. I enjoyed my few days of fame while I was treated like a celebrity, but these were soon over and forgotten.

I was very eager to talk to my friends from the hamlet. Our friendship was so close then and I hoped we would pick up where we had left off, but though we were very happy to see each other I felt there was a distance between us. We talked but the talk was of here and now. Even when the past came into the conversation, it did not bring us closer together. We found it difficult and somehow embarrassing to speak of our happy years. But when I looked into their eyes I could see the memories still there, but deeply buried and with no desire to disturb them for the time being.

One evening, talking to two brothers from the hamlet, I found out that, with other boys, they were delivering hay from up the river to stables in our camp. They suggested I join them after they had spoken to the foreman and I willingly agreed with their proposition. They promised to let me know the outcome in a few days. Meanwhile I thought I would investigate other kinds of employment. I knew that most of the people were working in the forest regardless of seasons. My father advised me strongly against joining the tree-felling gangs. This work was, he said, very hard and not well paid. He thought I ought to talk to the boys working in the forest, but with the horses.

At that time in the winter most of the activities in the camp were on the other side of the river. There, against the river banks, men were stacking logs in a kind of upside-down half pyramid. Two long logs were fixed vertically near the water level against which other logs were rolled down, until the top layer reached the top of the bank. Each layer was divided by two cross-runners to ease the load against the verticals, also making the rolling of logs that much easier. Towards the end of winter, the whole length of the bank was covered with log pyramids which were between 20 and 30 feet high. This work was highly dangerous and there were many accidents.

VITUNINO - LABOURS

What interested me most was the way the logs were transported to the river bank. When the trees were cut down, in winter or in summer, the logs were left where they fell. Only during the short summer were they moved and stored along miles of roads, which were just tunnels of cut-down trees. These roads were used only in the winter when the snow covered the tree stumps. Then sledge tracks were made, not dissimilar to railway lines, except these were sunk in the snow and, with constant use, the tracks were as hard and as slippery as ice. To transport the logs two sledges were tied together far apart to suit the lengths of logs.

The sledges were loaded up, man-high, weighing around six tons and made secure with four upright planks. Often the horse was unable to move stationary loaded sledges, for during the loading the steel covered runners froze to the icy tracks. On these occasions, men had to use considerable force to separate the frozen surfaces. Once on the move the speed

had to be judged very carefully with just enough acceleration to overcome small hills, but not more than a horse could control on the way down. When this happened the heavy sledges would push the horse forward, the horse would panic and go sideways only to be wedged against trees near the tracks. The load had to be in motion all the time; on no account could it stop on the road. The danger was the horse might not be able to restart, and sledges behind with too much speed could not stop in time to avoid a bad collision. There was a stop for off-loading, and again the speed had to be just right to stop at the exact spot. If the load went too far, a lot of time and effort was wasted pushing it back. The drivers were mainly boys in their twenties, who considered themselves the élite of the camp. There was no end to their stories of accidents and mishaps, and their earnings were the highest in Vitunino.

My rest days were nearly over and I had not heard from

the brothers. As arranged, I went to the administration hut and, after a long wait, I spoke to a Russian who was in charge of labour. At first he did not know what to do with me, but after some consultation with others he told me to report to the stables the next morning. The foreman at the stables was far too busy that morning to take notice of a boy, so I just stood there watching the horses being led out of the stables. There must have been at least thirty horses, all with riders and all harnessed ready for work. Gradually they rode away, leaving behind two or three poor-looking animals. That day and for the next few weeks, with other boys, I worked as a stable lad. We kept the place and equipment clean and tidy and ran some errands around the camp. Some days, with a sledge and a horse left behind, we would deliver water to the kitchen. The river was the only water supply and the inmates had to carry the water from the river in whatever containers they had. We dreaded the day when it was our turn to deliver the water to the kitchen. This involved taking a sledge with a barrel to the river, where you hoped there was already a hole in the ice. If not, you had to make one with an axe. With a bucket you filled the barrel and, however careful you were, you always got your clothing wet. Almost immediately your clothing would freeze which made you feel extremely cold and miserable. The errand was not made easier by a horse that had seen better days. To reach the top of the bank the horse had to pull the load up a steep hill. Often the animal had no strength and would stop on the way, when the sledge would slide back or go sideways. When this happened a horse was not able to restart and climb again. If you were lucky, some passers-by would give you a hand to push the load back up, but otherwise it meant half-emptying the barrel which involved making more trips.

Work and pay were closely connected. The Russians, in their wisdom, set a norm for different jobs and I was on the bottom of the ladder. My earnings and rations were very poor and I was ashamed of my small contributions towards the wellbeing of the family, especially on pay days while waiting in a small crowded room for your name to be called out. The

Russians always shouted out your name and the amount of money you earned. Mine was so small in comparison to the others that it made me feel small and depressed when I returned to our room. My parents were very supportive, saying that, after all, I was the recent arrival and pointing out that I was only 15 years old. Nevertheless I considered myself a failure for quite some time.

Not that there was anywhere to spend the money. The shop was rarely supplied with food or clothing, the two most wanted commodities. When this did happen, the news spread quickly around the camp, a queue would form and the goods sold out immediately. The kitchen food was allocated according to the work done and hardly ever in sufficient quantities. Families with grown-up boys fared better than the ones with girls or small children. The food itself was of a very poor quality and was constantly improved by provisions brought from Poland, which, after a year, were practically exhausted. Many families made contact with relatives left behind, who were able to send them food parcels and my family were among them. We received a number of parcels from our aunt and uncle, for which we were extremely grateful.

There were other ways of supplementing our meagre rations. Russians living in camps or villages not far from us would come knocking at the doors at night to trade food which they brought with them. They would bring eggs, butter and flour to exchange for items of clothing or jewellery. They would not sell it for money for we soon found out that in this part of the Soviet Union money had no value. These trans-actions were always done in secrecy, for they told us that if they were caught they would be punished just for talking to us. My mother was very glad that she brought with her my sisters' dresses, for these were in great demand. Such trading was common throughout the camp and people eagerly exchanged their possessions for food; only later did they realize how short-sighted they had been. In months to come these goods would become a matter of life or death.

Just as important was the food collected in the summer

from the surrounding forests and stored for the long, cold winters; all kinds of edible berries were made into preserves. Since we hardly had any sugar, they tasted very bitter, but that was the least of one's worries when one was hungry. Unfortunately the forests did not have mushrooms; apart from eating them boiled, these could be dried in the sun and again stored away for the winter. Although all kinds of fungi could be found in the woods, most of them were not edible. This did not stop some of the people experimenting with them, and I was told of one family who tried and all of them died of food poisoning.

The winter had still a few months to run and a lot of people suffered from what they called "chicken blindness". For no apparent reason they lost their sight; among them was my father. Those affected could be seen being led around the camp by others. What was worse, those afflicted were mainly middle-aged men, wage-earners, and of course the families, wellbeing suffered.

The only medical help was a Russian woman who was nurse, doctor, dentist and vet. She must have had experience of this Siberian ailment for very shortly everyone knew the cure, but getting it proved to be a problem. It could be overcome by eating liver in sufficient quantities. I seem to remember that some liver was available from the kitchen but only on the doctor's prescription and never enough for requirements. I also remember that the Russian women who were trading with us were asked for additional supplies. They were able to satisfy most of the demand, but this cost us dearly in rapidly diminishing goods. Nevertheless the cure was right and gradually the blindness disappeared.

About this time I developed toothache and for days I suffered terrible pain. I tried all kinds of remedies suggested by my parents and others, but to no avail. One night I could not take it any longer and in desperation somewhere I found a nail and with it I ran outside barefoot into the snow. I will never know why, but I put the nail into the cavity of my aching tooth and twisted. Of course this had the opposite effect and my toothache got worse. We all knew the tooth had to come out but who could do it? Reluctantly I went to see the so-called camp doctor and told her about my pain. Without hesitation or any anaesthetic she pulled the tooth out with something that looked like a pair of pliers. The pain during the extraction was excruciating but I was prepared for the worst to get rid of the toothache.

Snow was still on the ground when the two brothers from Chylin told me I could go with them on their next trip. One of the boys who usually went with them could not make it and I was to take his place. Early one morning six of us set out in three high-sideddouble sledges. All of them had done this trip many times before and had no difficulty in finding the way to our destination. To begin with we travelled on the frozen river, then we turned inland where, after a while, we found the snow-covered haystacks prepared the previous summer. We hurriedly loaded the sledges before darkness fell, for we yet had to find a cabin where we could spend the night. Sitting on top of the loaded hay we arrived at a small log cabin. There we lit a fire and sat around it to warm and dry ourselves. Soon the boys brought out some food given us for the trip and we ate and talked well into the night. Our conversation was never sombre; we joked and talked about the girls on the camp, but rarely, if ever, of the past. Our imagination was let loose when someone mentioned escape from this wilderness. This subject, I found out, was often discussed and lots of youthful plans were made, but always put off for the time being. We kept the fire going all night and slept on the hay covered with whatever we had brought with us. The next day we returned to Vitunino and offloaded the hay at the stables. Sadly this was the only hay trip I made.

There was no time for spring in this part of Russia. Since the summer lasts only three or four months the season begins immediately the snow disappears. The temperatures rise quickly, the river ice melts and suddenly the ground and trees are green. With the change of seasons came changes in camp activities. The most spectacular was the floating of logs stored during the winter. With great care the vertical logs were removed and with a thundering noise the logs stacked behind rolled down to the river. Some stacks, even when the vertical supports were taken away, would not collapse. In such cases the bottom logs had to be pulled out, which proved to be very dangerous, causing many injuries. Lastly, single logs that did not roll down, and there were many of them, had to be manhandled to leave the banks clear for the next winter. The river was full of moving logs floating down the river. Here and there men were stationed with long poles, mainly at the bridge to prevent any blockages.

That summer of 1941 the Commandant outlined the long-term plans for our camp and its occupants. Our future, we were told, was here and we would never return to our country. Poland did not exist. We were to stay here and build ourselves a village. To this end men with knowledge of building would start on new houses immediately. This announcement provoked mixed reactions. On one hand any improvement in our living accommodation was welcomed, but being told that our future was here was not so welcome. Not that we had any choice. But how dare they deny us the only hope we had to help us survive this nightmare. Whatever was said or planned, we could never admit to ourselves that this was the end of the road. This hope was constantly supported by dreams people had which, when translated by those who knew, always had profound meanings. Others quoted prophecies made years ago, reinforcing our dreams and, of course, there were signs in the skies with certain meanings, but above all there were prayers, not in large groups – this was not allowed – but in rooms where people prayed and sung hymns.

Summer also brought a change in my work. No longer a stable lad, I was to transport logs from where they fell to the storage area. This involved driving a two-wheeled carriage deep into the forest searching for logs cut the previous winter. On my own I had to lift one end of the log and put it on a carriage. Depending on the size of the timber, one load could consist of half a dozen logs or more, and then with ropes or chains I tied the logs to the carriage. Being a newcomer to this job, I was given a horse that nobody else wanted. After all, the other boys had been here a year or so longer and during that time they had picked the best animals and equipment. My horse was rather small, slow in movement and probably much older than the rest. I had no difficulty in harnessing him to the carriage but I could barely keep up with the main group on the way to the designated part of the forest. On the face of it the work did not look that difficult, but, as very often happens, it looked easy until you tried it. I had to find out the hard way what my horse was capable of pulling, how to tie the logs so they would not fall down, and then how to manoeuvre the load in the woods. For weeks I struggled to better myself, but the only thing I learned from the others was how to swear in both languages. The worst obstacles were the tree stumps, where my carriage often got trapped. I did not have the strength to lift the whole load, so I had to dismantle the timber, lift the two-wheeler over and then retie the logs. This sort of accident would happen many times during each trip and would lose me valuable time, hence less trips and less money, for, as everywhere else, there was a norm to be done. On many occasions, I remember, when things were going badly and there was no one to help me, alone and in desperation I would go down on my knees and looking up to heaven I would shout, "God! get me out of this hell. I will never ask you for anything else."

All summer I worked, dragging the logs without much success. Even later, working with different horses, I was unable to achieve the norm. On pay days, as before, I was ashamed of my earnings and felt a complete failure for providing so little. At times like these I would turn my thoughts to the happy summer days I had spent near my lake and river of so long ago. Only now and then would I voice my feelings, mainly to my sister Joanna when I would say, "Do you remember the . . .?" and so on, as if for an instant our recollections would obliterate the sorrow of the moment.

My father, even in Poland, was known as the local carpenter and smith, and it did not surprise me when he was chosen to work on the construction of the new huts. Under the supervision of the Russians, the work began early in the summer. It must have been going rather well because one day my father proudly announced that, in recognition of his contribution, he was to be given a cow heavy with a calf. It was unheard of to own a cow in a communist country and we were pleased with the news, especially my mother who was making plans as to what she would do with the milk when it came. The big day arrived. We had the cow and were told to expect the calf at the end of the summer. There was no shortage of grass and the cow was tied to a post or a tree on a long rope where she grazed happily.

Meanwhile the summer for us youngsters, even in exile, had to be lived and enjoyed. On a fine day after work the girls would parade in groups in their best dresses up and down the main thoroughfare. There, the boys would gather and engage in their usual horseplay, pretending the girls were furthest from their minds. If they met it was always in groups and only the older girls and boys would be seen walking in pairs; even then there would be a distance between them. I felt that serious romancing, if there was any, was not encouraged by parents, as it was not the right time or place.

Some days, I remember, there was a game of volleyball: where they got the net, not to mention the balls, I never knew. Since the maximum number of players was twelve there was not enough time for all the youngsters to take part and the game would continue until darkness fell. Occasionally we had a film shown in the large room next to the kitchen. It did not matter what the film was about, we went there to be in the crowd of young girls and boys. We were never taken in by the pure propaganda they were showing us, if anything, we were amazed at the naïveté of the films, especially when the films showed how wonderful life was in the Soviet Union, which we knew to be a blatant lie.

My memory fails me when trying to recall when and how we found out about the outbreak of war between Russia and Germany. When the news spread through the camp there was no other topic of conversation. For selfish reasons we all wanted Hitler to defeat Stalin and his régime. We had no knowledge of the situation in the West and, in any case, whatever happened there would not have any immediate effect on our plight. Our only hope at that time was that Germany would be victorious, which, especially in the eyes of the elders, was preferable to victory by Russia. Some of them remembered and compared the present division of Poland to Poland occupied and ruled by Austria, Russia and Prussia. For over a hundred years our country had been wiped off the map, until we regained our independence in 1920, and then only for twenty years. Most of our parents, though deported from Eastern Poland, had been born and spent their youth under Austrian occupation. History and their experience taught them that the most oppressive régime in divided Poland was Russia. Even in those days, Polish families were deported to the vast northern regions of Russia known as Siberia, a name feared through generations not only by Poles but by all the nations and races incorporated into the empire of the Soviet Union.

Exciting as the news was, the life in the camp did not change much. People still went to work and when the time allowed some families dug little vegetable gardens outside their huts. The youngsters, when possible, went into the forests to look for berries to be conserved ready for the coming winter. At about this time our cow disappeared one morning. The search around the camp produced no results and no one, when asked, had seen the animal. In the evening the search resumed: our family and our friends looked everywhere without success. Days went by and we more or less gave up hope, except for my father. At every opportunity he wandered off into the nearby forests, and sure enough one evening he came back not only with our cow but with a small calf. Apparently he had found them both not very far from our hut, grazing happily. My mother's wish had come true; she now had milk to add to our rations.

It must have been at the end of August, 1941, when I was told to go haymaking to feed the camp horses during the winter. Some of my friends had done this work the previous summer and from them I found out that we would be away for at least four days. On the day of our departure I joined a group of around a dozen boys and girls, mostly older than myself, and some adults. We were told that our equipment and food would be going up river in boats, while the rest of us would make the journey by foot. The boats duly arrived, rowed by older boys, and, after loading them up, we set off. Bunched together, we walked along the wooded river banks, led by the elders. Before long the group split up into a number of small groups, some into pairs of opposite sexes. It was becoming obvious that here was a chance for some of them to form closer relationships, alone and without parental interference. By the end of the day we had reached the cabin, which I recognized as the same one in which I had stayed overnight during my winter hay trip. Before darkness fell we lit a fire, prepared our evening meal and then made our way to the cabin for the night's rest. We all slept on the floor and by the time we had all found our places the cabin became quite crowded. All of us felt rather shy and uneasy that first night, only a few whispers here and there and then silence, except for the murmur of the river flowing nearby.

The next morning we collected our implements from the boats and the whole group walked further up the river. We had not gone very far when suddenly in front of us through the trees we could see large open spaces. On my left there was a small lake, on my right the river, and in between acres of green meadows. All was still and undisturbed and to me so very familiar. I wished I was on my own and could close my eyes and imagine I was somewhere else.

As days went by we got to know each other better and in the evenings gathered around the fire. There was friendly conversation, arguments and occasional laughter. The main topic had to be the war between the Soviet Union and Germany. The older generation got rather weary of us young-sters and our enthusiastic support for Germany's victory. In our naive and narrow view, we compared our present situa-tion with past history. When the powers occupying our country began to fight the end always brought us back our independence. History, we argued, repeats itself and we had no doubt that we would return whence we had come. To reinforce our deeply held views, someone would start a patriotic song and all of us would join in. On occasions like these we would stay outside well into the night. By the end of our stay we had completed what was required of us. The grass was cut down, dried in the sun and stored in haystacks ready for the next winter.

It was not more than a week after we came back from haymaking that the unbelievable happened. The historic event we all prayed for was to us a miracle that changed the rest of our lives. I was not present at the meeting called by the Commandant, but the announcement went through the camp like lightning: We were free to leave the camp and may, if we wished, travel south, where a Polish army was being organized.

Where exactly he did not know, except that it was somewhere in Uzbekistan. How to get there was up to us – he could not help – and when we left was our own decision. He still tried to persuade us to stay here in Vitunino, where we could build the village and settle down. How could he possibly imagine anyone wanting to remain here in this prison? For that was exactly how we saw it. Nevertheless, we saw great difficulties in undertaking such a long journey and our parents had to consider the matter very carefully.

Momentous as the news was, we had no idea at the time why we were being set free. Only much later did we find out the reason and how it came about. After the invasion of Russia the German forces were making rapid progress into Soviet territory and the Red Army were on the verge of defeat. Stalin realized that he needed help urgently and, since Great Britain was at war with Germany, the two nations, not surprisingly, formed an alliance. Close co-operation between Churchill, then Prime Minister of Great Britain, and Stalin was established. The immediate outcome was an offer from Great Britain to supply war materials to the struggling Red Army which was gladly accepted by the Russians. This unholy alliance did not escape unnoticed by the exiled Polish

Government in London led by General Sikorski. Through Churchill, General Sikorski initiated negotiations with Stalin for the release of all Poles, which included thousands of soldiers and officers kept in captivity through the vast expanses of the Russian empire. The ultimate purpose was to form a Polish Army, which, when equipped and trained, would eventually take part in the defeat of Hitler. Churchill at the time had considerable leverage, having in mind the badly needed supplies, and this I felt was a predominant factor in Stalin agreeing to Sikorski's proposal. In August, 1941, the agreement was reached and a general amnesty for Poles was announced.

The news of amnesty could be seen on the faces of all the camp occupants, but when the subject was mentioned there was much apprehension. The freedom given to us so suddenly and unexpectedly presented problems which became obvious during meetings at which future steps were discussed. The majority wanted to leave Vitunino immediately but there were some who thought it wiser to winter in the camp and make the journey in the following spring. The latter point of view made some sense considering that the summer was nearly over and there were so many arrangements to be made. If leaving the camp was delayed, they argued, the long journey south in the winter months was out of the question, especially since everyone was aware that the Russian authorities had refused to give any help in transportation or food. In the end those who decided not to wait for spring, among them my family and the other two families in our room, began to make plans for our departure.

It was agreed to make for Kotlas, the nearest railway known to us from a sad and not too distant past. From there we would travel south by train to Uzbekistan some 2,000 miles away. To get to Kotlas overland was ruled out: we could not walk and we had no transport of any kind. The river was the only option left to us, and the only way was to float on rafts. Not that anyone had any experience in building rafts or what to do once it was in the water and time was not on our side. If we were to go before winter we had to move fast. The final

outcome was that the men would start on the rafts immediately, while the women and children would gather as much
food as possible from wherever they could.

Our room decided to build one raft to accommodate all
three families, six grown-ups, ten children and our possessions. All rafts, and there were many of them, were to be built
some distance up-river where suitable timber was to be
found. I remember my father and two other men coming back
late at night for days, tired but happy with the progress being
made. Often they would discuss the problems encountered
and remark about other rafts that were being built differently
and at different stages of completion. Since there was no blue-
print for design, the strength and speed of construction
depended on how skilful the teams were. Once, I remember,
the men returned at the end of the day more excited than
usual. They had heard gunshots not far away and suspected
that the Russians were trying to frighten them into abandon-
ing their preparations for departure. If that was true, and we
never found out who was behind it, the perpetrators
misjudged our determination. There was no going back. Our
minds were made up. In the meantime food presented
considerable problems: there just was not enough to save for
the unknown future. All our efforts produced very little.
Whatever bread was bought or saved was dried and stored
in sacks. Trading with Russian women added some flour and
grain, but overall the supplies collected were only sufficient
for days rather than weeks.

I did not see the rafts during construction and had no idea
what they would look like, but when I first saw them I was
deeply disappointed. Ours was small, mostly under water and
there was no superstructure, which I thought was essential
for us to live and sleep in. I did not voice my misgivings but
I doubted if this raft would take us anywhere. It could not
have been more than 20 foot long and 12 foot wide, with two
cross-layers of logs tied together with pliable twigs and some
wooden dowels here and there. There were two large oars at
the front and rear, mounted on fork-shaped uprights, with no
guardrails, just an open platform. My father and his two

friends must have noticed our puzzled faces but assured us that the appearance was not everything and, God willing, we would be safe on the initial stage of our long and uncharted way south.

9

South By River

On the day of our departure early in September, 1941, there were dozens of rafts ready to sail. They did not differ greatly at first glance, but what mattered most was the strength of the construction, which, as we were later to find out, was crucial. We loaded our possessions on to the middle of the platform where the women and children were to stay. The sides were left free for easy walking. These rafts were the first to leave Vitunino; others, not yet ready, were to follow. We promised to keep close together during the voyage in case of any mishaps, when we would help each other. We hoped to arrive in Kotlas in one group; there the next stage of our journey would have to be negotiated.

That was indeed a day to remember. We were happy just to be on the move. It did not matter where we were going or whether we would make it or not; we were escaping from captivity. Most of the people in the camp came to see us off. There were tears and farewells to those who had decided to stay the winter and would follow us. Especially sad goodbyes were exchanged between families from our hamlet, but we all were sure we would meet again somewhere in Uzbekistan if not this year then definitely in 1942. With last wishes for a safe journey and the usual waving of hands, one by one the rafts were pushed away from the river bank and we were afloat. Bunched together, slowly and with care, we manoeuvred our rafts through the first

obstacle, the supports of the Vitunino Bridge.

We were free, and yet we felt that at any moment we might be caught and returned, even punished. Not knowing exactly how to control the raft, the men watched carefully the effect achieved when the large oars were moved from side to side. We soon realized that we were too close to the other rafts and, since all of us were novices, there was danger of collision. We had long poles which we could use to push the raft away from the banks or the other rafts, but there was no need for this. Before long the togetherness we had promised each other became impossible. By luck or by skill, some rafts found the fast-flowing side of the river, while others encountered slack water or had difficulties with steering. Soon our convoy stretched over a considerable distance. The men were fully occupied with the oars, and we boys (there were four of us) kept close to the long poles on both sides of the raft to push away from danger. The women and younger children were huddled together in the centre around our possessions.

During the first day the river provided us with a fast flow and we were making good headway. The steep banks were covered with trees and there was no sign of human life. There were many bends and towards the end of the day we lost all visual contact with other rafts. The light was failing fast and we had to find a place where we could tie up for the night. Eventually we stopped against a high bank, clear of trees, giving the appearance of meadows beyond. After securing the raft as best we could, and now in darkness, some of us climbed the bank to explore what was above. To our surprise we could see some distant light, but what really caught our attention was what looked like cultivated land. We decided to investigate further and some of us walked on a short way to find fields of growing rye. We picked some of the spiked heads and returned, showing our find to the grown-ups. Our parents realized that here was a chance of supplementing our food supplies. For the next few hours we gathered as many heads as we could and brought them back to our raft. We knew very well that we were thieving and if caught who knows what might happen. With this in mind we vowed to get up very early next morning and escape unnoticed.

The next day, just before sunrise and with mist all around, we were on our way. If we thought we were the first on the river we were mistaken, for there were already rafts passing us, with whom we exchanged the latest news. Other rafts were still tied to the banks with occupants fast asleep. So far, from what we saw or heard, all was well, with no mishaps of any consequence. The river had been kind to us. We now could see more open land with occasional buildings, but we paid little attention. For, apart from the men at the oars, we were busy with the previous night's harvest. We crushed the spiky heads in the palms of our hands, separating the grain from the husk. Carefully, we would blow away the light waste and store the clear grain. When the task was completed, we were very pleased with the amount of additional provisions, which we were to find invaluable in the weeks to come.

Once we were on the move we very rarely stopped. Only when my mother decided we should eat something hot we would select a suitable length of bank and stop. The fire would be lit, over which all kinds of containers would be pushed to boil whatever food we had, but never in sufficient quantities. We all knew that we had to use our provisions sparingly, for our long journey had just begun. Most of it was still in front of us. Each time we stopped we took the opportunity to look around, if by any chance there was some food to be found, not necessarily for immediate consumption but for future use. This preoccupation with food was then and later our constant obsession, regardless of the means employed to get it, be they lawful or criminal.

So far we were making good progress. The banks were becoming low and less overgrown with gentle slopes terminating here and there in sandy beaches. At the same time the river was getting much wider and very shallow in places. Navigation was not easy. Now we had to work hard to keep our raft in deep water. Our long poles were in constant use, not only to gauge the depth but also to push away from the shallow areas. On a few occasions, I remember, when taking a bend we would come upon a raft stranded in the middle of the river and the occupants waving their arms for us to keep to one side or the other. We were very grateful for the information given, but were unable to help them; there was no way to get to them. If we stopped near them we would be stranded ourselves, and if we stopped on the bank we could not get to them. Sadly we would leave them in their predicament and glad that we were still on the move. But our luck had to run out and, shortly, in spite of our efforts, our raft hit one of the many shallow spots. It swung around and we were beached. No amount of pushing with the long poles could dislodge us, if anything the fast flow of the river was taking us towards a now-visible sandy bottom. There was no time for discussion. We had to decide quickly on our next move before the raft sustained any damage. At first only the men jumped into the water, but, after brief unsuccessful struggles, some of the women and we four boys followed to give a hand. We had to push the raft against the stream and, when in deeper water, to guide it away from where we had grounded. Of course once the raft became lighter with most of us off it, it moved forward and wedged itself harder than before. No matter what we tried failed miserably. Our clothing was wet, the water was cold, we were cold and we were losing our tempers. The struggle went on for what seemed like hours; then someone suggested we should use our long poles as levers. This proved to be more effective. While one side was held fast we levered the front, step by step, against the flow of the water. Slowly the raft was swung into the stream and we scrambled back on to the raft.

Exhausted, wet and very cold, we steered to the nearest bank we could find. There we rested, dried ourselves and even recalled some amusing moments. The men examined the raft and found no serious damage except for some logs which had to be re-secured.

Rested, we resumed our travels, but not before promising ourselves to be more careful in future. Needless to say, before the end of our journey we did run aground once more but this time we were wiser and refloated our raft without undue complications.

Before night fell we reached a wide stretch of open country with the river winding as far as the eye could see. In the distance we could make out a hill with numerous huts on top and some lower down near the river. We were making for what we thought to be a small village where we hoped to spend the night. Suddenly our attention was drawn to what appeared to be a fence across the river and at the same time we heard an angry murmur of water. Before panic set in, we noticed a small opening in the centre of the fence but the panic was not over. We were to one side of the river and if we did not move fast enough to the centre there was no doubt we would collide with this barrier. Furiously, we rowed and pushed the raft towards the gap and just managed to squeeze through. Only when we looked back did we realize what this obstacle was. The villagers had constructed a wooden dam, leaving a small gap in the centre, where at times a net was laid with a long tail to catch fish. Consequently there were two different water levels, forming a small waterfall in the gap over which we were lucky to pass safely.

As we approached the village we could see other rafts already tied to the bank at the bottom of the hill. We came alongside with warm greetings and smiles of recognition and relief. All of us were eager to talk, especially of the events of the last few days, and what had happened to the others. In no time the villagers, curious as to who the visitors were, came down to talk to us. We were told where we were and informed that, provided all went well, we should reach Kotlas the next day. What was more important to us, the village had an eating house where we might get a meal. We did not waste any time. We climbed the gentle hill and had no trouble locating a long building with a kitchen. Timidly, we walked into the large room with many windows overlooking the river, and of course the customary portrait of Stalin and red banners proclaiming the glory of communism. There were not many people about and we had no difficulty in finding a table near one of the windows. While the men went to the kitchen to ask for food, the rest of us looked through the window and admired the sunset and the spectacular panorama below us. To this day I remember the unspoilt beauty of this Siberian wilderness, the well-trodden hill sloping down towards the river and the meadows meeting expanses of woodland at the edges of the horizon.

Eye-catching as the view was, we kept glancing in the direction of the kitchen where my father and the other men were deep in conversation. They kept pointing towards us and we suspected that the presence of so many was working against us. Only later did we find out that the sight of hungry young children had tipped the balance and we were offered hot soup and some bread. Feeling much better after an unexpected but very welcome meal, we left the eating house and returned in darkness to our raft. Anticipating a hard and exciting day ahead, we all retired for the night, promising to start early the next morning.

We had no knowledge of how many rafts were in front of

us or behind, but presumed we all were making a steady progress. We hoped that, given a day or two, our group would assemble in Kotlas as planned. On that last fine morning on the river, after all the chores were done, one by one the rafts were pushed away from the banks and once again we were on the move. The wilderness that was so apparent before now gave way to vast open spaces with occasional settlements of varying sizes. Glad as we were to see houses and people, to whom we waved, we were well aware that sooner or later we would come across another wooden barrier, similar to the one encountered the day before. We realized the danger these obstacles presented, and to avoid any mishaps a constant watch was kept, especially when approaching a village.

Our fears materialized quickly when, in the distance, we noticed timber logs sticking out of the water at awkward angles. Coming nearer we recognized with horror that the logs were from one of our rafts wedged against the dam fence. Disturbed as we were, we could not dwell on this distressing sight as our own survival was at stake. Only after safely negotiating the obstacle did we look back with sorrow and a prayer for the occupants whose fate we never discovered. Then we saw the cause of the disaster. Some of the timber barriers had sustained damage or were left in disrepair, leaving large gaps along their length. Consequently, a number of openings faced the oncoming rafts. Unfortunately, except for the middle portion, other gaps, with the posts just under the water level, formed a trap where a raft, once lodged, could not be refloated. In no time at all the craft would fall apart. Considering the fast flow and the two different water levels I had no doubt that each one of us had a thought as to what had happened to the occupants but no one dared to say it aloud, not at that moment, maybe later. Such were the unwritten laws of survival. As the day wore on we came upon other rafts damaged and abandoned. We passed them in silence, knowing that there, but for the grace of God, we too would end up.

Though we did not know it at the time, this was to be our

last day on the river and we were mentally and physically exhausted. If we had had to travel much further, there was no doubt that we would have to have a long rest, but as the day was coming to an end it was obvious we were approaching a large settlement. On the horizon we could see many buildings much bigger than the huts we had passed before. There were multi-storey brick structures and towers; but above all we noticed regular puffs of smoke, which after a while we recognized as train engines. Now we knew we had reached Kotlas, the relief and joy of safe arrival could be seen on all our faces. We steered towards a row of warehouses where trains were moving about. Coming closer I was sure the long buildings were the same I had seen through the window of the police station, when I was there on my own not so long ago. How different my second visit was. Now I was with my family, just passing through in the hope of getting back to my birthplace. This hope, at the early stage of our travels, was very real. Going south, though not of our choosing, was somehow only a small diversion in the great plan which would eventually lead us back to Poland, regardless of the outcome of the war.

We were not the first to arrive in Kotlas. In the failing light we could just see the frantic waving of hands visible against the steep banks of the river. Coming closer we recognized some of the rafts from our group, waiting for the rest of us as previously agreed. With care we manoeuvred our raft to the edge of the river and, with the help of others, we beached our floating logs for the very last time. All of us were overjoyed with our success at safely negotiating what we thought was the hardest part of our journey and it showed when we warmly greeted each other. On occasions like these everyone wanted to recall the events of the last few days. This could have continued well into the night, but all that, we decided, could wait until the morning. We all needed a good night's rest. Only a few days had passed since we had left Vitunino and here we were partially retracing our steps, but now without a Red Army escort. We were free, yet still uncertain as to our future and our final destination.

We slept on the raft and in the morning looked about us at our surroundings. There were numerous steamboats not far from us, moored to a timber platform and what looked like never-ending loading and unloading between boats and wagon trains above. The high bank prevented us seeing the town and, since there was no easy way up, we were quite content for the time being to stay on our rafts. After all our group was not yet complete and we were expecting more rafts to arrive. We decided to wait until all of us were assembled here before further arrangements were made. In the meantime my father and other men left to investigate the possibility of obtaining some food. For those left behind, mainly women and children, there was not much to do. Our possessions were packed ready to move, but there was no hurry. We suspected that it would be days before the next part of the journey. The only way we could travel south was by train and, considering that the Soviet Union was at war, we could foresee many difficulties and delays.

Now and then our heads would turn down the river from which direction we were expecting the remainder of the rafts to come. I did not want to miss the excitement of the reunion, but my curiosity got the better of me. I had to find out whether the warehouses along the river banks were the same ones I had seen from the window of the Police Station on my way to Vitunino. Convinced that the rafts would come much later in the day, I climbed the bank. To my left, as far as I could see, were railway lines crowded with goods wagons. On my right I could see rows of buildings and warehouses, on both sides of what I thought to be a railway station some distance away. Undecided as to my next step, I stood there watching the wagons being shunted, mostly by Russian women.

Choosing a relatively quiet moment, I carefully, and practically on all fours, managed to get to the other side of the tracks, only to be confronted by a high wall in front of me. Having got that far, I was not going to give up. There must be a way to see what was beyond the wall. I turned left and walked between the wall and the wagons towards what appeared to be a light at the end of the tunnel. There the wall ended and I came to a large timber yard. There, among the stored logs, I came at last to a wide road with numerous buildings on the opposite side. Standing there, partially hidden from the street, my eyes turned left to a long brick building a few storeys high. There were entrances at both ends with many windows in between. My heart missed a beat as I stared at the right-hand doorway with several steps in front. I could not read the signboard above the door, but there was no need. I had no doubt it was the Police Station and that that was the doorway I had walked through to the sledge which took me to my family just over six months ago. I did not recognize the window of the room I had stayed in and I did not wish to go any closer. My curiosity was satisfied. I turned back and, with uncertain emotions, retraced my steps and rejoined my family who by now were a bit worried at my disappearance.

In my absence my father and the other men returned with the news that sometime in the afternoon we might be able to get some food. Nobody had showed much interest in where I had been. They had other more important matters on their minds. My little escapade was so personal and of no significance, but I was pleased that I had made the effort.

By the time we had collected and eaten the food from the station kitchen the long-awaited rafts began to arrive. One by one they came, each greeted with great enthusiasm. Some of the rafts were showing considerable damage, with loose or missing logs, the occupants very tired, but overjoyed that they had made it. We did not have to ask what had happened; all of us knew, and in varying degrees had experienced, similar horrors.

The next morning there we were around a hundred of us, more or less evenly divided between grown-ups and children. Further meetings took place and, not long after, a number of men left us to go to the Railway Station to arrange whatever railway transport was available. For the rest of us there was nothing else to do but wait for the outcome of their enquiries. Occasionally we were visited by some Russian officials and other curious onlookers, but satisfied with our explanations, we were left in peace. Hours went by and there was no sign of our delegation returning. Expectations were high; otherwise, we thought, they would have been back. When they eventually showed up, we crowded around them to hear the news. As we listened, one could judge by the smiling faces that the news was encouraging. There was a possibility of hiring two wagons, similar to the cattle trucks that had brought us here. When? They did not know, but if a certain amount of money changed hands it could be quite soon. Most of the money, I understood, would be pure and simple bribery of the officials. The amount was of no concern to us youngsters; we left the group happy in the knowledge that we would soon be on the move again. Long after, our parents were still in deep discussion. When it ended the money in their possession was collected to pay for our transport south. Here for the very first time, if I remember correctly, our destination was mentioned. We were heading for a town called Tashkent in Uzbekistan.

Not wishing to delay our departure, our parents made the necessary arrangements as quickly as possible. Now there was nothing to do but be patient and wait upon the slow-moving Soviet bureaucracy. We lived and slept on the rafts; once a day we collected our rations from the station kitchen, always soup and sometimes bread, and never in sufficient quantities. The soup we got was either fish or cabbage and the only way one could tell the difference was by the smell. To help matters we kept a few fires burning, around which assortments of pots and pans were placed containing the soup and such added ingredients as we still had. My mother performed near-miracles to make this water concoction more palatable and to last longer.

The food, all of us realized, would play a crucial part during the impending train journey. Our hard-saved money almost gone, we had no alternative but to sell or exchange our last possessions. There were two ways of trading with Russians: one was to call at nearby houses, but mainly we dealt with people who came to see us. It soon became known that we were willing to exchange our goods for food. As in Vitunino,

Russian women brought whatever little they had – eggs, flour, grits and other provisions – for which we gave them items of clothing. One of the most treasured possessions was dried bread kept in a sack for real emergencies. My mother, I remember, was very reluctant to open it and how right she was. We were not starving yet.

Days went by. The middle of September, 1941, was upon us, and so was the cold weather. We longed to get away from this place of our exile. Constant bothering of the officials paid off in the end and one day two wagons appeared on top of the bank not very far from us. When told these were ours, we eagerly went up to see our future accommodation. The trucks were of the same type that had been used for our deportation from Poland. The difference was that this time we were to occupy them of our own free will.

10

Train South

After several trips up and down the river bank we took our belongings and settled down in our wagons. This time there was no barbed wire on the windows and the doors were not bolted behind us. We busied ourselves making our wagon as comfortable as possible for what we knew would be a long journey. No one expected immediate departure. After all, there was a war going on and we must have been at the bottom of all priority lists. When, eventually, an engine appeared and we were hitched to a goods train our spirits lifted. Soon the train moved and the pleasant but monotonous sound of iron wheels on rails filled the wagon. To this day this sound has a relaxing effect on me, regardless of circumstances.

Through the windows and the open doors we could read the names of the stations as we passed. They were small and the names meant little to us. Only the position of the sun indicated that we were travelling south. The countryside was still just expanses of woodland with small villages here and there. Frequently a discussion would take place about the route we were travelling and the length of time our journey would take. Had we had a map we would have know that we were going south towards the town of Kirov.

There, and later wherever we stopped, a certain pattern was established. Our wagons would be taken to some remote siding and left for an unspecified time. As soon as we were

TRAIN SOUTH - KAZAKHSTAN

stationary most of the grown-ups, equipped with all kinds of containers, left in search of food. This often developed into a race for fear that there would not be enough for all. For us youngsters there were many duties to perform. Apart from food, we collected whatever wood we could find. What wood we did not use immediately we stored away for later. Less pleasant, but a very useful function we youngsters performed was to scrounge or even steal whatever we could find of use to us. We searched all the waste ground, open buildings, sheds and wagons, but rarely with much success. Soon it became obvious to us that anything worthwhile around the stations was either locked or guarded by soldiers. We needed to extend our activities further afield, but up to now we had been afraid of being left behind and had limited our range to within eye contact of our wagons. This caution was to be disregarded sooner than we expected. The distance became of no consequence as the search for food became more desperate.

107

For some 1,000 miles we travelled south from Kirov through densely populated and industrial parts of the Russian Republic, the largest Republic of the Soviet Union. Our progress was very spasmodic; often we went very short distances, with long delays at the stations waiting for a suitable goods train going in our direction. The only consolation was that at least we could feed ourselves from the station kitchens. These occasions were greatly appreciated by all families, for not only was our hunger partially satisfied but, more important, we were not using our own supplies. During this part of the journey we were joined by other wagons occupied by Polish families going south. By the time we reached the second largest Republic of Kazakhstan there were a dozen or so wagons full of hungry and confused Poles escaping from various parts of Siberia.

Probably no one remembered, but sometime during this part of our travels, on 22 September, I was 16 years old.

Kazakhstan, though still part of the Soviet Union, was to us a completely different world. The countryside became barren and flat with all shades of brown everywhere. The rare green areas we came across were settlements with small white buildings scattered around. There were hardly any big towns and for hours, sometimes days, we travelled through vast open spaces with few signs of human life or animals. When we did come into contact with the local people, they were of a different race, culture and language, with dark complexions, high cheek bones and narrow eyes. The men looked hard and unapproachable, but appearances are often misleading, as I later found out when I came to know them better.

Ahead of us lay another 1,000 miles through Kazakhstan to Tashkent, our destination. This part of the journey was far more eventful and difficult than the previous 1,000 miles. As before, our journey was often interrupted for no apparent reason and the train would stop, sometimes in the middle of nowhere. We never knew for how long and this led to all kinds of incidents. Since food was not available at the small railway stations we were passing, we had to rely on our own supplies. As soon as the train stopped my mother and the other women would start a fire and cook something hot. If there was no wood stored in the wagons, we youngsters would go into the fields searching for whatever would burn. Since trees were very rare in this region, what we came back with were mostly dried-up shrubs and bushes. There, and later on, the most common fuel we found was a kind of overgrown heather which, when dried, lost its roots and was blown all over the open spaces by the wind.

With no time to lose, fires would be lit and, to save the fuel, each fire would be closely packed with food containers for boiling. Women would stand around them keeping one eye on the fire and the other on the train in case it moved. The rest of us were not far away if we were needed. What happened when the train suddenly moved is vividly imprinted on my memory. The reader has to imagine the panic. Leaving our precious food behind never occurred to anyone, nor the danger involved. Hot, even boiling pots and pans were removed from the fire and hurriedly transported to the wagons. All kinds of injuries were sustained, mostly burns, when running towards the moving train. Even when you reached the open doors the containers had to be lifted four or five feet to the floor level of the wagons, gaining speed all the time. Now you had to scramble aboard yourself as best you could. Often you were pulled up by those inside, getting bruises and scratches all over your body in the process. We thought that some of the train drivers derived a certain sadistic pleasure from seeing our mad scramble onto the moving train.

We were now escaping from the cold northern weather. Here the days were sunny and warm. Often the heat in our crowded trucks was unbearable, especially for those on the upper bunks, even with the two sliding doors open. The misery was made worse by the primitive personal hygiene and lack of any medical help. Most affected were the elderly who in extreme circumstances were left behind on some railway station with the hope of hospitalization. Progressively our appearance deteriorated; our clothing was wearing out and by now whatever we had had spare had been sold or exchanged for food. The clothes we had on hardly covered our thin bodies and, had it not been for the warm climate, who knows how many of us would have survived.

Despair and depression could be seen on all our faces. Our parents must have suffered terribly to see their children hungry and in rags. I remember my mother and father on one occasion deep in conversation. It was not loud enough for me to hear, but I knew the subject, for shortly after our belongings were examined and the last of our possessions of value were removed. This was my mother's fur coat which I was surprised to see still with us. At the next railway station at which we stopped I noticed my father leaving us with the fur coat under his arm. Some time passed and there was no sign of him returning, my mother anxiously looked in all directions. This was not unusual, as in the past he had always managed to come back just in time, but when the train began to move and we still could not see him our anxiety turned to panic. Sobbing, my mother gathered us children together; my three sisters and I were hardly able to speak. Young as we were we realized the seriousness of what had happened and with heavy hearts we cuddled close for comfort. What would become of us without him was unthinkable.

For a number of days we travelled on without him. Our friends knew of our misfortune and tried their best to console us, but the prospect of facing the unknown without our father was something we could not accept. My mother, I remember, had that faraway look at that time which I knew from before. She was praying. Everywhere we stopped our eyes would search for the familiar figure to appear and we would wake from the nightmare.

We never knew whether he was ahead of us or behind us, our journey was so unpredictable. On many occasions when we stopped other trains went through. He could have been on any one of them.

Among all the stations we passed or stopped at, one was exceptional, and a picture of it is still with me. After the usual shunting we were left in some remote sidings and I made my way to the main building. The wide platform had a number of raised flower beds full of shrubs and plants in full bloom. Against this beautiful flower arrangement stood a one-storey station building painted white with a large arched central entrance and similar-sized windows in the long frontal elevation. The whole layout was tastefully put together and spotlessly clean, yet all to my mind was spoiled by an enormous statue of Stalin. There he stood with his arm outstretched in the centre of it all, completely out of proportion to the immediate surroundings. It could have been at this station or one shortly after – my memory fails me here – that my father rejoined us, but I remember that when I returned from my usual scrounging forays he was there. I missed the happy reunion but seeing my father with us was enough for me to shed tears of joy. What had happened to him was something we always dreaded. To sell an article such as a fur coat required time. He called on many houses, but finding someone who wanted it and could afford it was not easy. He knew the sale had to be made and when he had found someone who could pay in money and some food he hurried back to find us gone. Catching whatever trains he could, he eventually caught up with us. Listening to my father's story I was surprised to see him so calm, as though this was just a minor mishap. Yet for us the days without him were full of apprehension.

No doubt the money from that sale had a lot to do with what happened to me shortly after. Some of it was given to me by my father who told me to buy some food when we next stopped. I wish he had never made that request for the outcome shamed me greatly at the time, and does so even now when I recall it. On my own I left the train and walked the streets near the station, finding nothing. I ventured further and found a large open market. There were many stalls with various kinds of produce but none that I thought suitable for my family. What caught my eye was a plentiful display of walnuts. To this day I do not know why I bought them. That was bad enough. What was worse was that I ate them all. Even worse, on my return I told my father that the money had been stolen. How could I have been so selfish? I must have known my parents and sisters were as hungry as I was maybe more so, and the shame of that day will haunt me for the rest of my life.

October, 1941, was upon us when, exhausted, starved, dirty and in rags, we arrived in Tashkent. I remember, just before we reached the town, that there was a lot of talk warning us against thieves who supposedly were everywhere on the station. We were told a thief might have a bottomless suitcase which he would put on top of yours and walk away with both. It occurred to me, as I listened to this, that we had nothing left worth stealing. But we decided to stay in our trucks while some of the grown-ups left us to investigate the situation and report back. After all, we had been told at the outset that Tashkent was our destination and here we were. Unfortunately, no one could tell us what to expect at the end of our long and perilous journey.

11

South With Tears

Over a million Poles had been deported to the Soviet Union and thousands of them were converging on Tashkent in the early days of the amnesty. The station was overflowing with people all looking for guidance and answers to so many questions. Where do we go from here? When and how to join the Polish Army? What will become of the women and children? If we thought that our misery was at an end we were badly mistaken. The Russians were fully occupied in their desperate fight against the German forces. It was becoming obvious that our presence was a needless problem to be got rid of as soon as possible. Polish organization at that time was in its infancy and could only operate within the limited means provided by Stalin and his regime. Nevertheless, the rare sight of a Polish uniform was the only spark of light in the prevailing chaos.

We were told that after a few days, to relieve the congestion, the families would be dispersed for the time being to various *Kolkhozes* (collective farms) in the district. Soon our turn came and, travelling through Samarkand, we were taken to the banks of the River Amu Darya. There, with hundreds of others, we were abandoned to a fate nobody could foretell.

The sight that greeted us was becoming increasingly familiar. Families were scattered in groups, sitting on the grass around their meagre possessions. Here and there a fire was burning, surrounded by women, closely watching their boiling pots containing whatever food they had. Hardly anyone moved to see the newcomers and I suspected tiredness was not the only reason. Gloom and depression overtook us all and replaced the high hopes we had had at the beginning of our journey south. This grim picture of all these unwanted people contrasted sharply with the pleasant scenery around us.

The wide majestic river was not unlike a narrow lake, set in a flat open terrain. Both banks rose gently from clear, slow-moving water. The green grass extended as far as the sloping ground, beyond the greenery there was nothing but desert. This vast expanse of sunburned land was dotted with occasional shrubbery which, as in the past, was eagerly collected for firewood. Here under the open sky we were to spend several days just waiting. We slept on the ground wrapped in anything we could find, for the nights were getting chilly, although the days were still very warm.

Here also I saw my family for longer periods by the light of day. Before, while travelling, most of the time we saw each other only in the semi-darkness of the trucks. Now what I saw disturbed me greatly, especially my mother. Although for the latter part of our journey she had been rather withdrawn and did not move too much, I presumed she was just tired like all of us. Her face was much thinner and her skin was an abnormal colour, but most noticeable were her eyes. They were sunk deep into her head with dark grey circles round them. She was still able to perform her motherly duties but at a much reduced pace and rested whenever she could. My father was most attentive to her, which only reinforced my suspicions that she was seriously ill. On the surface my father appeared to be healthy but he could not hide his concern not only for my mother but also for my older sister, Lucia. She was never a picture of health, always with a pale complexion and looking like a beanstalk. To make matters worse she now had difficulty in swallowing her food. Being so weak she was not of much help to my mother and it fell to my younger sister Joanna to do the housework for the family. More often than not she was the one to fetch and carry, with frequent help from myself. Daily, both of us would wander deep into the steppe looking for fuel for the fire. None could be found within easy reach, for demand far exceeded supply. During these walks our conversation was always of the happy childhood days at our farm in Poland and what we would see and do when we returned. The only person in my family who was not affected by the misery we were enduring was my youngest sister Jagoda. She was barely five years old. Unaware and innocent, she played games with the smile of the pure. She was also the only one to survive with no memories of the two years spent in the hell created by Stalin.

The days near the river dragged on and our provisions were practically gone. We ate very little and hunger and starvation was plainly visible on the crowded banks. Mercifully the day came when we were given some rations and told to prepare for imminent departure. Not long after our transport arrived in the form of several long, flat-bottom iron barges pulled by a lone steamboat. The barges were huge open freight boats most likely used for carrying cotton, the local staple produce. Along the top edges there was a narrow unprotected gangway with a number of flimsy ladders leading down to a large open area. Into these barges hundreds of people disappeared with their belongings. From the gangway where I spent most of my time, looking down I could see a human hive, but barely alive. Hardly anyone moved or spoke and the crowded floor scarcely allowed for the sick or exhausted to lie down. Frequently I would turn towards the place where my family was and there see the sad, weak eyes of my mother.

Another river journey, but very much unlike the one from Archangel. This time I had no need to hide from the cold wind and frost; this time I was escaping from the Siberian imprisonment, but, above all, this time I was not on my own.

Before long the barges were on the move, going upstream towards a range of mountains bordering Afghanistan. Gradually the flat, desolate land gave way to hills and later to steep gorges of white stone with black vertical streaks. We were now entering the wide valley of the River Amu Darya in the Soviet Republic of Uzbekistan. The further we went up the river the more our apprehension grew. In the opinion of many we were losing contact with the Polish Army organization, our only salvation. Others were resigned to their fate. After all we had no choice.

The days on the river came to end when we reached a small secondary valley extending northwards. The barges stopped against a sandy bank on a very hot day and we disembarked. Presently, as if in a mirage, a convoy of *arbas* (high, two-wheeled carts) appeared, pulled by oxen and accompanied by numerous camels. We loaded our belongings and with some difficulty found enough room for those who could not walk. Among them was my mother who looked very poorly and had to be helped on to the cart. Unexpectedly, I was told to sit on a laden camel with a warning to hold tight. Without much thought, I did what I was told. A few moments later I was very grateful for the advice given, for when the camel rose the movement back and forth was of such elevation and force that anyone not prepared would have fallen. Overcoming the initial shock, I found the camel ride very uncomfortable, comparable to being in a small boat on choppy water.

Once again we were on the move, travelling on a sandy road winding its way through occasional settlements. Between these and hills were expanses of irrigated fields covered with endless rows of cotton bushes. The road was full of all kinds of vehicles, carts, camels and donkeys all loaded with large bales of cotton. It seemed as though the whole local population was engaged in one way or another with this harvest. In spite of all the activities, our presence aroused considerable interest. We were asked many questions, but I doubt if any of our answers satisfied their curiosity.

Towards the end of the day, in the failing light, we arrived at a small village. The scattered houses were mostly made of mud with small windows and protruding flat roofs. There were a number of big wooden sheds and other more substantial buildings flying the red flag with the hammer and sickle. As we were going through the village one by one the carts and camels veered away from the main convoy and

disappeared from our view. Our turn came soon and we parted company from the others and, after a while, stopped in front of what looked like a wooden stable. The large doors were open and we were shown a raised clay floor in the corner. This, we were told, was to be our temporary home — an empty shed somewhere in a remote and God-forsaken part of that evil empire! For how long? Will anyone ever find us? Does anyone really care? But these thoughts were left unsaid for fear that, if voiced, they would depress us even more.

Separated from other Polish families, and feeling abandoned by the whole human race, our spirits dropped to the lowest level yet. Although my sister Lucia was slowly recovering, my mother by now was so weak that we had to carry her up on to the platform. We prepared the bedding and made her as comfortable as possible. My father looked very worried and told us that in the morning he would go to the village to find help. That night I lay awake for hours with all kinds of thoughts going through my mind. Most of them concerned the misfortunes that had befallen my family and the uncertainty of our future. Also, for the first time, I admitted

to myself that I would probably never see Poland again.

None of us slept well and we were up early in the morning, apprehensive of what the new day would bring. The shed was very old and in a bad state of repair, built of timber with a solid clay floor. The walls were full of holes and the high roof looked as though it would collapse at any moment and come crashing down on us. The building had clearly been used to store cotton, but now it stood empty and neglected, surrounded by cotton fields on all sides. The nearest houses were some distance away, reached by overgrown narrow lanes.

Whatever plans the local officials had for us was of no immediate consequence. Our only concern was my mother, who was now very ill, yet we rarely heard her complaining. As early as he could, my father left us with many instructions as to how to cope in his absence. For hours we sat there, never far from our mother, eagerly awaiting his return. In the late afternoon he came back in the company of a stranger and we were told to go outside. A while later we heard that our mother would be taken to hospital the following day. The news cheered us up a little, but what we heard shortly after did not please us at all. In order to obtain food we were to take part in the harvest, picking cotton. The well known communist slogan "Who does not work, does not eat" applied here as everywhere else.

Sometime next morning we had a visitor, who showed us the fields in which we were to work, how to pick cotton and where to store it. He also gave us each a kind of double-skin apron which formed a large front pocket when worn, into which cotton was placed when picked. We began our labours close to the shed in case the hospital transport showed up. We had hardly started when an *arba* arrived and we rushed back with mixed feelings, glad that she was going to get medical care but sad that she was leaving us.

Most likely my mother did not know what was happening as she hardly opened her eyes. In a blanket she was carried out and placed on top of the cart. Confused and of little use, we four children stood there watching. My father came over to comfort us and to tell us he was going with our mother and should be back later in the day. While he was away we were to continue working. I can still see my sisters and myself, bewildered, standing there in the middle of nowhere waving goodbyes to the disappearing *arba*. How could we not think the unthinkable – would we ever see our mother again?

Left alone, we tried to do what we were told but our minds were elsewhere. Our eyes scanned the horizon for signs of our father and our fingers were cut and bleeding. Cotton picking required certain skills which we did not possess. The outer cover of a ripe cotton bud is divided into several hard petals, each with a sharp pointed tip. Almost every time, when trying to pull out the white fluffy cotton from the bud your fingers would come into contact with the sharp point. Our fingers suffered badly and our efforts at cotton-picking were practically worthless. Only the return of our father brightened the miserable day. Deeply worried, he gathered us around him and did his best to lift our sagging spirits. Hopefully, he told us, our mother should be back with us in a week or so, if all went well. Our gloom partially dispelled, we retired for the night, perhaps to dream of better days.

The food we received was dependent on the results of our work, but it never amounted to more than some bread and various oats, sometimes flour. My two elder sisters, Lucia and Joanna, took over the chores and duties normally done by my mother. Poor girls, their work did not end in the fields, and on our return to the shed they were still busy well into the night. Jagoda, my youngest sister, came with us everywhere, even cotton picking, not that she contributed much, but her presence often brought a smile to our sombre faces.

The days dragged on, broken at regular intervals by the arrival of a local man on an *arba* to collect the cotton we had picked. On these occasions my father would get into conversation with him and the predictable outcome would follow. From among our depleted possessions an article would be selected and eventually exchanged for food or money. His contact with the Uzbekis (natives of Uzbekistan) was useful in more ways than one. Apart from eagerly sought information about other Polish families in the village, unofficially my father used to arrange visits to the hospital. None of us children went with him, but each time he went he brought back the news we wanted to hear. Our mother was getting better and shortly, if the improvement continued, she would be back with us.

A fortnight or so went by when, unexpectedly, my father returned from the hospital on an *arba* with my mother by his side. Happy as we were, we soon noticed that all was not well. Although she looked better and the joy of seeing her children was there on her face she was still very unsteady on her feet. My father, aware of the situation, assured us that, given enough rest, my mother should soon be back to normal. Unfortunately fate decided differently. The badly needed days of rest never came; we were to be on the move again.

October, 1941, was coming to an end and we were making

our way back to the river: the same people, the same convoy, on the same roads, but now with a certain optimism. Surely, we thought, the only reason why we were being moved was that somewhere something had been arranged to end our exile or at least make it bearable. With these hopes we were taken to the river bank to await further transportation. Here families and friends met again, greeting each other warmly, eagerly exchanging experiences and the latest news. The main topic, of course, was where we were going and what awaited us. The rumours were endless but the one mostly accepted was that we were to settle in camps around the Polish Army now being organized. This Army, when ready, would join the Red Army and the Germans would be pushed back from the Soviet Union and eventually from Poland. Only then would we be able to return to our homes. It all sounded so plausible and logical. Other rumours, amongst them one speculating on our evacuation to a neighbouring country, were rejected as wishful thinking.

Without much delay the iron barges came and soon we were going down the river, retracing our journey of not so long ago. Still in high spirits, we disembarked at exactly the same spot where we had begun our journey upstream. Experienced by now in this kind of travel, the families quickly settled down on the river bank anticipating an early departure. No one was unduly worried about food shortages. After all, we thought, our movements from now on must have been carefully planned. Even the absence of officials, be they Russian or Polish, did not disturb our mood of optimism. This hope was so strongly implanted in our minds that we were quite prepared to stay and sleep in the open, go without food if necessary, provided the salvation we all expected was at hand.

The days were still warm, the long summer in this region lasting until the end of the year. The nights, on the other hand, were getting noticeably cold, compelling families to sleep huddled together for warmth. As days went by and no one took much interest in our plight, the situation became critical. The lack of any information as to what would become of us was bad enough, but the lack of food made us desperate. Most of the families had used up the provisions they had and, even if they could have exchanged their last possessions, there was nowhere and no one to trade with. We youngsters still went far into the open steppe in search of dry shrubs and some fires were lit, but now the flames were not so closely packed with pots. Even those boiling did not necessarily contain food in the acceptable sense of the word. It became quite common to see women walking along the grassy banks, searching for something on the ground. They were looking for various plants which they considered edible. Those picked were mixed with whatever small creatures lived there, then boiled and eaten! The mood of optimism had vanished rapidly and changed into a grim battle for survival. Our lives in this so-called Communist Paradise were one continual struggle for food, just when we thought we had escaped from the hell of the north. Now we faced starvation in the south to a degree unknown before.

Disaster was not far away for the hundreds of men, women and children living in appalling conditions on the banks of the Amu Darya River. Would the voyage across Russia so eagerly undertaken only a few months ago now end in tragedy? When, how, and who was going to rescue us from this nightmare. Resigned and disillusioned, people sat quietly in family groups staring into empty space.

The day we woke up from this nightmare came suddenly, but many days passed before it finally ended. At first the sight of several *arbas* on the horizon did not arouse much interest. Only a few of us made the effort to stand up and watch, but as the carts came nearer many more got up, anxious to discover the purpose of their visit. No doubt the majority were hoping that at last some urgently wanted food was to be distributed; if so, they were mistaken. The Uzbekis stopped some distance away, then came over to be immediately swamped by the crowd. The eerie stillness that had hung over us for so long was now broken by many excited voices all talking at the same time. To most of the questions asked they had no answer, but the reason why they were here was

ABANDONED - AMU DARYA

simple. They had orders to collect as many families as they could and distribute them to various collective farms in the district.

The news was received in disbelief and disappointment could be seen on all faces. How could this be! We had been through all this before! Surely it was time we were given some peace and rest somewhere under Polish authority. But our fate was not in our hands and we could only watch as certain families were selected for the first departure. Before long, the goodbyes said, the loaded *arbas* moved off in the direction from whence they had come. Slowly the crowd dispersed in the knowledge that a similar relocation awaited us all.

For days afterwards, sporadically and in various numbers, the *arbas* would come to take away more families. We soon noticed that priority was given to able-bodied families. Those with sick or old members, or even small children, were avoided. My family, with three others, probably somewhere in the middle of the prevailing order, departed early one

123

morning on a warm and sunny day. Room was found on the top of the *arbas* for those who could not make it on foot, among them my mother, who was visibly getting weaker.

The heavily-laden oxen-pulled *arbas* made slow but steady progress across the open Kara Kum steppe and by midday, our small convoy found itself in a thinly populated province of Uzbekistan, travelling on soft sandy roads. The heat of the day did not help our tired bodies. We were hungry, exhausted and in urgent need of rest. The sun was still high in the sky when we reached a small town, situated on two hills with a shallow valley between. The tired oxen came to a small square where we were told we could have a badly wanted break.

The main street where we stopped was unusually wide, lined with many trees on both sides. Behind them stood well-separated houses, most of them showing signs of age and neglect. The pavements shaded by the trees were quite busy with people going in and out of numerous shops, cafés and eating houses. The other hill, across the valley, was more like a small village with a large open market in the middle. The overall appearance of this picturesque countrified town was so pleasant and so unlike anything I had seen before that I only wish I could remember its name.

To hide from the blazing sun some of us found a resting place under a tree where, after a while, my father came to see me. Pushing some money into my hand, he told me to go to the market to buy something to eat. On my own, I left the group and began walking towards the other hill. I stopped here and there to satisfy my curiosity, not realizing how much time I was wasting. The market was crowded and busy and there were many goods on display, mostly water melons, nuts and all kinds of fruit. I always found it difficult to chose the best buy for the family and this time was no exception. I wasted more time before I made my purchase and then, slightly concerned that I had been away for so long, I hurried back to find the square empty.

Surely they would not go without me, I thought. I looked up and down the road, but the hills restricted my vision. I rushed in all directions but there was no sign of them. With my heart beating faster and faster, I ran back to the square, hoping someone would tell me what had happened. Few people I asked had witnessed their presence, and as to where they had gone they had no idea. Since I had not come across them when returning from the market, I ran in the opposite direction, to the top of the nearest hill. Breathless, I stood there, my eyes searching for any movement on the roads, hardly defined on the bleak and sandy horizon. My hopes rose for a moment when I saw a cloud of dust on the distant hill. I watched carefully for anything familiar, anything that would tell me it was them, but there was nothing. In any case, whoever they were the distance was such that I did not think I could catch up with them.

Why, oh why, had it happened again? Why me? Why am I here alone on this hill, undecided as to my next step? I sat down with my head in my hands and tears rolling down my cheeks on to the hot soft sand.

I knew I had to go back, but there was no hurry. There was no one waiting for me. If only I could turn the clock back, but how far? Where would I want it to stop? Not surprisingly, my mind went back to that period of my life when I was in exile and alone. I recalled the shattering experience of my homecoming in February, 1940, my journey to Lesopunkt, Archangel and the river that froze. Then the hardships of a long walk in the Siberian winter and near death at the end of it. Dramatic as those twelve months were, I was always with my compatriots who played no small part in my survival, but here I was among strangers, people of a different race. For some reason I was afraid that my face and appearance would be easily recognized as that of an outsider.

Most of that day I spent on the outskirts of the town. Since I had some food with me there was no necessity to go there in the daylight. I thought it wiser to wait until the evening when my entry would be less conspicuous. With some caution and in the failing light, I walked slowly up and down the main street. No one paid much attention to me, except for a few youngsters who turned their heads, knowing

instantly that I was not one of them. The older generation, and there were many of them, were mostly engaged in conversation, taking little notice of the children running around. I passed many open doors leading to smoke-filled rooms which I presumed to be cafés or eating houses, but I did not have enough courage to go inside. As the night wore on these places became very crowded and only then did I feel brave enough to enter one of them. I selected what I thought was the largest eating house at the edge of the valley with extensive outbuildings at the back. The spacious room was dimly lit with some tables and chairs along the outside wall. The rest of the room had a raised floor covered with rugs, on which people sat in groups eating from a large communal dish. The place was packed, noisy and full of smoke. Here I felt safer, lost in the crowd.

I knew that, sooner rather than later, I had to find somewhere where I could spend the night. I left the crowded room and in the darkness made my way along the sloping side of the valley to inspect the outbuildings I had seen before. Facing me was a long lean-to structure partially walled, lit only by the windows of the main building. I went up and looked inside into what unmistakably was a shed full of discarded rubbish. At the extreme end I could make out shapes of cardboard boxes. There, I thought, was my place for the night. Afraid to make any noise too early, I went back into the street, to return later when the town was asleep.

Gradually, in the darkness, the street became quiet and empty. Returning to the place I had selected for the night, I noted that some of the cafés, although closed for business, were still partially occupied by people lying on the floor. This puzzled me and I promised to look into it at a later date. Meanwhile, I had things to do. I had no difficulty in finding the spot, but, now without any light, I had to feel my way around. Very carefully, with as little noise as I could manage, I flattened some of the boxes and laid them down in the corner. In addition, I found some newspaper out of which I formed a pillow, leaving enough to cover my body. Satisfied with my improvised bed, I lay down, covered myself as best I could and prepared for what I knew would be a rough and uncomfortable night. Sleep did not come easily, I was cold and my thoughts always came back to what I would do tomorrow and thereafter. At the outset I decided I would stay here and wait. I was still convinced my father would come back and look for me. Even if I attempted to go in search of my family, where would I go? Who could tell me where they were? I had no intention of asking the local officials or the police, since my faith in the communist system had long since vanished. Other more disturbing thoughts entered my mind: How long could I stay in hiding? Where could I turn to for food? I had no money and no prospect of earning any.

In spite of all my worries, I must have had some sleep, for I woke up with the rising sun, though still sleepy and rather cold. There was no doubt in my mind that the coming nights would have to be spent elsewhere. I left the shed with no definite ideas for the day, except to keep on the move, hoping this would make me less noticeable. I went in the direction of the market where there was much activity in preparation for the morning trade. It occurred to me that I might be given some food if I offered to help, but shyness prevented me and in any case I still had some food left over from the day before. I left the market and walked on, always pretending, more to myself than to others, that I had a specific purpose.

I followed the road beyond the built-up area, then turned back, crossed the valley and came to the hill where not many hours ago I had sat crying. I realized I should be better off around the market and the square for these were the most likely places my father would go to look for me. I also knew I could not keep up the pretence for days on end and, finally, as always, there was the problem of food. I promised myself to be more positive the next day, but for now I was prepared to keep moving.

Throughout the evening I was never far away from the eating house which I had previously visited. I kept a watch on the comings and goings through the open door. Now and then I went in for a few seconds, as though I was looking for someone. Late into the night, when all was quiet and hardly any light from the windows I entered the room. When my eyes became accustomed to the dark interior, I saw many men sleeping on the raised floor. Careful not to disturb anyone, I found a space near the edge where I lay down and shortly fell fast asleep.

Morning came much too soon for me. I had slept well and I was warm, though slightly stiff. Judging by what had happened, last night's occupation by the sleeping men seemed a normal occurrence accepted by the proprietor. He must have known most of them as he greeted them by their names. I felt sure he spotted me, being the only young boy and the only stranger among them, but I did not want to attract attention to myself, so I left the room, relieved to have avoided an encounter with the proprietor.

That morning I went straight to the market, where already many *arbas* and camels were arriving fully laden with goods. Deep down I knew I had to make some kind of contact with one of the traders and this made me very nervous to say the least. Unsure of how and what to do for the best, I walked slowly, trying to catch somebody's eye. At long last I made up my mind to make my timid approach. I stopped near a buxom middle-aged woman, dressed in a black cloak and accompanied by a small boy. They began to offload the cart, paying little attention to the people around. From time to time she glanced at me and, seeing me still standing there, after a while she gave me a faint smile. Encouraged by this recognition, I came closer, asking her if I could be of any help. She gave me a long look, puzzled by the presence of this strange boy. Anticipating her questions, I explained briefly the reason for my being there. She listened patiently with an expression of disbelief. Probably she had never heard of the country I came from. Nevertheless her motherly instinct, I suspected, prevailed and she nodded to me to follow her. Together we carried her goods and laid them out on the rickety stall. For my efforts she gave me several rolled millet pancakes for which I was very grateful. Thanking her for her generosity, I did not dare ask her if she would be there the next day. I did not want to press my luck too far.

Most of the remainder of the day I spent between the market and the square, hoping to see a familiar face. I was disappointed but not in despair when, at the end of the day, I was still alone. After all it was only the third day since we had parted. Maybe tomorrow.

Evening came and I was beginning to feel more secure walking the streets. As on the night before, I slept more or less in the same spot, but in the morning the unexpected happened. The proprietor, an oldish man, stopped me before I could leave the room. If I was frightened I need not have been; his face was kind, without threat or anger. His curiosity was obvious. He wanted to know why a small boy like me was alone and, of all the places, in Uzbekistan. We had a long chat and he was clearly anxious to find out more details about my life in the Soviet Union. He listened with deep sympathy and understanding and often interrupted me to express his hatred for communism. As great a hatred, if not greater, was directed towards the Russian people. He had nothing in common with Russian people, who, in his opinion, oppressed and exploited his nation. The bitterness he felt was expanded and reinforced in the days to come, for, before we parted that morning, he asked me how I could manage to feed myself. I told him I was destitute and he suggested that I come back in the evening when the place was busy to help him around the kitchen. Naturally I thanked him warmly for his kindness. And, if I did not, I should have raised my eyes with gratitude to whoever up there was watching over me.

By the time I reached the market most of the stalls were already trading. The woman I had helped the day before was not there and no one seemed to want my help. Aimlessly I wandered through the market, always on the lookout for something to put into my hungry mouth. Often I would select a stall kept by a woman and would stand gazing into her eyes until I was offered some food or told to go away. There were times when I asked or begged for it, and there were rare occasions when I took what did not belong to me. When I left the market it was only to go to the square, just in case he was there.

Being on the move most of the day, I was tired and glad when the time came for me to go inside the eating house. I had no difficulty in locating my Uzbek benefactor, who took me to the small kitchen at the back of the house. There I spent the whole evening keeping the fire going, washing up and generally helped in food preparation. For my efforts I was given a hot meal and, feeling much better for it, I retired for the night to the familiar raised floor. My fourth day of separation from my family came to an end on a more hopeful note.

Another week or so went by before we met. I was already doing my rounds in the market when I saw him coming up from the valley. I ran towards him with my arms open. After an emotional reunion we sat down on the ground and talked of all that had happened to us since we had last seen each other. I heard how heartbroken he felt at leaving me behind, but he had no choice. I understood the reasons. He could not abandon my sick mother and my sisters. He described the journey which ended late that night in some *kolkhoz* miles away. All four families were housed in one isolated mud house on the top of a hill. There was no work to earn any money and the food rations were barely enough to survive on. In turn I went over my experiences of the days apart, asking him at the end when and how was he going to take me back with him. His answer did not come straightaway. He sat there very thoughtfully and, when he spoke, his words were carefully chosen.

"Why don't you stay here? You would be much better off here than where we are, and I will come for you when the time . . ."

I did not let him finish. I was hurt and astonished that such a thought could have entered his mind. The subject was painful to both of us and, my father realizing this, did not pursue it any further. Deep down I knew he meant well, but how could I see it? Only time would show how right he had been.

Although I had been in that town for over a week I had not known that there was a railway line only a few miles away. A short journey by train had brought my father there and now we were making our way to the station for the return trip. As we crossed the valley we came to the eating house where I had spent the nights. My father knew all about the house and the old Uzbek. We could not go without saying goodbye to him. We walked into a room partially empty, as it always was around midday, but we were told that the old man was not there. The only thing I could do was to leave a message with many thanks. I walked away with fond memories of the old man with his thin face and the colourful Uzbek cap on his head.

The railway station was not very big, with several small buildings and one platform. Since the journey was not very long, my father told me we would travel without tickets and warned to keep near him at all times. As soon as we saw the train approaching we went to the side without the platform and, as the train was moving out, we ran and jumped onto the last wagon. Several stations later, after successfully dodging the ticket inspector, we got off and began walking in the direction of the *kolkhoz* where the rest of our family was awaiting us.

November, 1941, was half-gone, the weather was still fine and warm and we were nearing the hill with the mud-house. It was not until I reached the top that I was able to appreciate what my father had tried to tell me only hours ago. The *kibitka,* as those primitive mud houses were called, was so tiny that I could hardly believe it accommodated four families. Around me as far as I could see there was nothing but desert, except a small village at the bottom of the hill, but still some miles away. We turned towards the *kibitka* to see a group of children sitting quietly against the front wall. Among them I recognized my two younger sisters Joanna and Jagoda, who ran to greet us.

Together we entered a dark room, partially sunk into the ground, lit only by two small windows. The length and width was just enough for four families (eight grown-ups and fourteen children) to lie down like sardines, leaving a narrow passage between the feet and the wall. The dark interior, with a low roof and rough dirty-looking walls, contributed to the grim atmosphere, which was reflected on the faces of those present. Immediately on my entrance I saw my mother and my elder sister sitting to my right. She did not get up to greet me, and as we hugged each other I could not help noticing her eyes, which told me she was not getting better. Then I went around to say hello to the two families, Tomczynski and Jaworski, neighbours from Poland, and one family named Zakoscielny who I did not know.

Weeks of deep misery followed. There was no work, only endless waiting and hoping for a better tomorrow. Our parents pretended there was some purpose in whatever they were doing, moved like shadows, rarely speaking and never smiling. Gone were the days when their possessions would be exchanged for food. Now they had to rely on meagre food rations brought from the village. To say we were hungry is an understatement, we were slowly starving. Children fared better; our parents saw to it by denying themselves the precious little they had. Even so, all of us were by now aware

of the grim situation and our normal exuberance was put aside.

Only days after my arrival a meeting took place during which the parents discussed our situation. The main topic was the fear of being forgotten and the total lack of any information regarding the Polish Army organization. In the end a man was selected who would travel by train and, hopefully, somewhere along the line would meet someone in authority. A kind of collection was made to help him on the way and he left us with our best wishes. A day or so after he came back, not exactly with what we wanted to hear. The main station was still crowded with Polish families escaping from the north, awaiting a similar fate to ours. The Polish Army had established a number of bases, the nearest one at a town called Guzar. The advice given to him was that all families with small children should stay together wherever they were. Since the oldest child in our group was around 17 years, we had no alternative but to stay put and await further developments. To that end our address was noted with a promise of a future contact.

The news, if anything, depressed us even more. Now we knew that our struggle for survival had no end in sight. My father and the other men began to look for some kind of employment, not even for money but for whatever food they could obtain. The nearby village was the obvious place, and there, eventually, my father was employed as a part-time carpenter. His work was mostly repairs to the houses for which he received some flour and bread. I remember once he brought a goat's cheese, never seen before. It was white in colour and resembled a cricket ball in size, and was just as hard. We had to break it up into small pieces and hold them in our mouth until they dissolved with a strong but pleasant flavour.

Days went by without much happening. We still went deep into the steppe in search of dried shrubs and twigs as fuel for our small stove inside our *kibitka*. During these walks we often came across a flock of sheep, unlike any others I had seen. The back end of the animal was extended by a flapping tail in the shape of a small cushion. This cushion was apparently valued by the Uzbeks as a supply of lard used in the preparation of local dishes. Now and then we would wander far enough to see trains go by in the distance. How could we not dream of being on them speeding away from this wretched land?

One night I remember waking up to the sound of people talking in half-whispers. I lay there intrigued and somewhat scared, unable to understand what was going on. I heard voices calling on the spirits of dead Polish leaders to answer various questions regarding our future. Questions like will we escape from Russia? Will we return to a free Poland and when? Each question was followed by the sound of an object being moved on a hard surface. When the sound momentarily stopped I would hear someone say a letter of the alphabet. I could not restrain my curiosity any longer and sat up to see my father and others grouped together round a board on the floor. In the dim light I could see their outstretched hands with fingers touching what looked like a saucer. After each question the saucer would move from letter to letter forming in the end words of a sentence. Although I did not know at the time, I was witness to a ouija board seance. Fascinated as I was, I suspected the saucer was manipulated by one person who had prepared the agenda in advance. Most of the answers, I seem to remember, were rather optimistic, and not exactly accurate, for we never returned to Poland as the ouija board had predicted.

From the hill where we were, one day we noticed unusual activities in the village. It seemed as though the whole village had gathered outside, dressed in their fineries to celebrate what could have been an Islamic Holy Day. We could not resist the temptation of going to see what was happening. Towards evening several other boys and I shyly approached the outskirts of the village. There was a small fire burning over which a large cast iron pot was suspended and attended to by women, while the men sat around in small groups. Soon each group was served with a bowl from which men began to eat with their fingers. The Uzbekis could not help but notice us standing expectantly at a discreet distance. Presently they called us over, inviting us to sit and eat with them. The bowls were filled with boiled rice and mutton spiced with yellow powder. We copied our hosts and ate with our fingers, which was probably our first taste of curry. During the meal, though they knew about us on the hill, they asked us many questions and listened to our answers with great sympathy. Needless to say, we were very grateful not only for the meal, but also for the kindness shown to such a pitiful-looking lot as us.

Even today, when I close my eyes, there are the moments I cannot erase from my memory, even after so many years. The emotions evoked are deep, painful and very real. The picture of my mother sitting inside the *kibitka*, weak, hardly able to move and with deep-set black eyes. The image is very vivid and unforgettable.

Christmas comes but once a year and 1941 was no exception. That year there was no cheer for us and thousands of Polish families now in the south of the Soviet Union. Living in such primitive conditions, and being so isolated, the passing of time had no real meaning. I often wondered how we knew the dates. We had no newspapers or radios; how did we know it was Christmas? I cannot remember anyone talking about it; there were no preparations nor any visible change in our dreary existence. Yet when Christmas Eve came our *kibitka* remembered the evening. Soon after darkness all of us went round to wish each other good fortune for the future. In normal circumstances this was done with a communion wafer. Here we carried in our hands a small piece of bread, carefully saved by our mothers for the occasion. Each time you faced someone and exchanged good wishes you broke the bread from the other person, ate it, and then embraced warmly. This old custom, especially among the families, was always a very touching moment and was more so on that evening. Many tears were shed, because of the desires and hopes expressed, which mostly concerned our survival and return to our homeland. But very little was left of the traditional Christmas Eve. We had no Christmas tree, no presents to open, and no midnight mass to look forward to. What we were still able to do was to sing our old Polish carols. As hard as we tried that evening, our voices broke down too often under the weight of memories of other places and other times.

Only days after Christmas my father took me aside for a talk, which probably changed my life for ever. He pointed out the desperate situation we were in. My mother, he told me, was seriously ill and he hoped she would soon go back to hospital. He expressed fears of what might happen to us all if we had to stay there much longer. Why don't I go to the nearest Polish Army base, he suggested, where I would have a better chance of survival. He had no choice but to stay behind to look after my mother and sisters. How ironic, I thought, after all we had been through and my nightmare journey to be with them. Were we to be separated again? At first I refused, but in the end I saw the sense of his advice and agreed to go.

No preparations were necessary for my departure. There was no need for packing; I had nothing left. By now all of us were destitute. I bade my farewells to the other families, then with a heavy heart I said my goodbyes to my father and three sisters, all the time promising to return if things did not work out. Had we known that it would be years before we met, our parting would have been far more painful.

Finally I went to my mother. We sat there with our arms around each other hardly knowing what to say. Tearfully, we said our goodbyes, her sad eyes following me until I went through the door of the *kibitka*. I never saw my mother again.

12

From Russia For Ever

Alone, with no definite plans in my mind, I made my way to the railway station. My immediate destination was the town of Guzar, where, I was told, was the nearest Polish Army base. How to get there concerned me since I had very little money. My father gave me some roubles, but I made up my mind not to waste them on a railway ticket. At the station I found out the time and direction of the Guzar train and walked across the line. There I sat down on the grass opposite the platform, where several men with similar ideas were already waiting.

When the train came we made ourselves ready. One by one we jumped on to the last wagon as the train was moving out. I knew my journey would take only a few hours at the most. With that in mind, I did not follow the others and stayed at the end of the train. Before long the inevitable happened. The ticket inspector entered the carriage and I was caught. I did my best to explain who I was, where I was going and why I had not got a ticket. He did not show any anger but in a loud voice, mostly I thought for the benefit of the onlookers, he ordered me off. At the next stop, as I was leaving the train in his presence, he told me quietly that what I did next was none of his business. Taking the hint, I got back on as soon as the train moved on. For the rest of the journey we avoided each other and eventually I arrived in Guzar.

As I stepped on to the platform I could not help noticing

soldiers dressed in the uniforms of the Polish Army. What made them so conspicuous were the four-sided caps they wore, like no other Army. Smiling broadly, I went to the nearest soldier and spoke to him. He was there for exactly that purpose and he told me how to get to the Guzar site. I walked across some fields to the outskirts of the town where I was directed to a big brick building. I walked into a large hall which I took to be a disused cinema without seats. The room was crowded with boys of various ages, mostly seated or lying on the floor. The absence of any commotion usually associated with so many boys was unreal, almost nightmarish. The overall picture was of lost or starving children wearing oversized rags. I walked across the room on to a stage where a man behind a table interviewed me. He asked me a lot of questions about my family, education, how I got there etc. After making some notes he gave me a few blankets and told me that for the time being I was to stay in the hall.

At all times of the day and night there were new arrivals and the hall was getting overcrowded. One day my name was called out, together with those of other boys, and we were taken through the town to a site near the river. Along the gently sloping banks there were many tents covering large dug-outs. Most of the tents were already occupied by Poles of all ages and both sexes. One of the empty tents was allocated to us, a group of twenty or so boys of similar age. We were all strangers, except for the two Buja brothers who slept next to me. The three of us became firm friends; the younger one, Felek, proved to be a true friend later on when I badly needed one.

Many boys, by the time they reached Guzar, were showing signs of starvation. Like walking skeletons they moved slowly with deliberate steps, their eyes bulging out of their bony faces. Their main preoccupation was food, prepared by the field kitchen, where they spent most of the time. The hot meals did not differ much from what we were used to. Soup and bread was the most common food, sometimes boiled rice with mutton, but it still was not enough to satisfy the starved

and hungry boys. Not surprisingly, the shrunken stomachs could not cope with the sudden increase in food consumption and diarrhoea affected the majority of us. The sanitary accommodation was practically non-existent, so human excrement was everywhere, and the stench hung over the site like a cloud. We were told that a typhus epidemic was spreading rapidly through the camp. We were forbidden to drink the badly polluted water from the river, yet the supply of water from elsewhere was insufficient to satisfy our thirst. Many of us continued to use the river water not only for drinking but also for washing ourselves, our clothing and utensils.

Tragedy struck our tent only days after we moved into it. One morning we woke up as usual with the exception of one boy named Ptaszek. At first we did not take much notice. Maybe he wanted to sleep a bit longer, we thought. When, after a while, he was still lying there covered with a blanket,

140

we tried to wake him up. One of the boys pulled the blanket off and to our horror we discovered that he was dead. No one had heard anything out of the ordinary that night. He had died peacefully in a hostile land after a long trek, but among his own. I cannot remember any cries of sorrow, or any signs of shock. We just accepted this sad event, numbed by our two years of struggle for survival.

With half of January, 1942, nearly gone the winter came to Guzar. The snow came down thick and fast, forming deep drifts between the tents. The cold weather made our lives more miserable. None of us had any warm clothing and for additional protection we wrapped ourselves in the blankets, under which we slept, sat and moved about. At about that time I began to feel weak and feverish. I did not mention this to anyone for fear of being separated from my newly-made friends. On the way to the river site I remembered seeing a tent with a big red cross painted on it. I decided to find the tent and seek advice.

The ground was still thickly covered with snow when I found the tent on the outskirts of the encampment. From the distance I could see the unforgettable scene, as if in a dream. Against the whiteness of the snow, there was the large red cross from where a black dotted tail ran down a small hill towards me. The tail was the human queue waiting to enter the only tent where medical help could be found. The black dots were the sick, some standing and some sitting, completely unaware of what was happening around. I joined the queue, which hardly moved, but I noticed that those sitting in the snow kept still. As we moved up I realized why they were so still – they were dead or dying. I was appalled by the indifference shown by all those present. How could we stand by and not help another human being? Confused by what I saw, I left the queue and returned to my tent. Was that picture of what I thought to be inhuman behaviour another rule to be observed in order to survive?

Shortly after this our tent and some other boys were called out for relocation. Once again there was no need for any preparation; we had no belongings; we were ready to move

GUZAR

at any time. Under the supervision of a Polish soldier, we were taken to a railway station and then on a train to a small town called Wrevskoye. During the walk and the short train journey I did not feel at all well. I had a fever and ached all over but not for a second did I consider complaining, I was not going to be left behind.

Another short walk from Wrevskoye station and we found ourselves in what looked like an army camp. We entered the camp through a pleasant wooded area where a field kitchen was situated. In front of us there was a wide area, similar to a parade ground. On all sides there were rows of wooden huts and we were led to one of them. Presently a Polish Officer came out and welcomed us warmly. Here, we were told, was the main assembly centre for boys like us run on army lines. The Sergeant was introduced as the Commander in Charge of the Company we were allocated to. He took us across the parade ground to a hut which was already partially occupied by boys. Inside both long walls were lined with wooden bunk beds. Feeling very tired, I selected the nearest bottom bunk and lay down to rest.

Reluctantly I got up and went with the others for our first meal. I ate very little, still pretending there was nothing wrong with me. The next day I hardly got up. I was not interested in food, and I knew I was getting weaker. My friend Felek noticed I was not well and came over to ask me what was the matter. I was sure, I told him, that, given a few days' rest, I would regain my strength. He was not convinced and told me he would report me sick. My fever must have been high, for in a way I was glad he left me. All I wanted was just to sleep.

Vaguely I remembered people around me, trying to lift me up from my bunk and then nothing. The next recollection I had was of someone shouting at me and shaking me to wake up. Why are they bothering me, I thought, I was so comfortable where I was. Slowly I opened my eyes to see a woman standing over me in a room I did not know. I was lying on the floor, in a long barrack divided into small recesses by timber screens. The recess I was in was full of boys laid out on the floor side by side. From what I saw and the way I felt I suspected I was in hospital. Apart from the extreme weakness and fever, my body, I felt, was not touching the floor; I was floating on air. I was given something bitter to drink and then left in peace.

Gradually I discovered that I had been brought there unconscious and had lain in a coma for a few days. We were all suffering from typhus, rampant throughout the camp, as it had been in Guzar. The hospital, or rather quarantine hut, for that was what we were in, was isolated from the main base and no visitors were allowed. The boys were at different stages of the epidemic; some were just able to walk and others like myself were too weak to move. The women who looked after us were marvellous, more like mothers nursing their own children. They were responsible for the recovery of many of us. In my case Felek, my friend, played a substantial part in my return to health.

I was still very ill; I could not walk; I had no appetite for food, except a burning thirst. At that critical moment Felek showed up. One day he appeared at the window. Unable to come inside, he did his best to cheer me up from afar and asked me if there was anything he could do. My only desire was for a drink and I told him so. From then on there was not a day that he was not there at the window with a bottle of *kwas,* a dark brown drink made from fermented yeast and bread. I later found out that he had to go to the railway station where *kwas* was sold at street kiosks, and of course he had to pay for it. He was also waiting for me when, after several weeks, I eventually left the quarantine hut, and he helped me back to our quarters. I am sure that it was the drink and also his friendship that kept me alive, when so many other boys died.

The unit I was in had around a hundred boys between the ages of 12 and 15. Ours was the youngest company: there were, I would guess, another four similar units with older boys. Even in those early days we were introduced to army life. We stood on parade in two rows according to height, the tallest boys at the head of the parade. We marched in rows of four as was the Polish Army custom. We may have acted like young soldiers but at that time, because of our pitiful clothing, we never looked like them. Imagine our joy when we were told that we would be issued with new uniforms. The day came when we discarded our rags, our heads were shaved and we went through a de-licing spray. Then we queued up to receive British battledress, complete with shirt, cap, shoes, underwear and many other items. It did not matter at all that most of them were too large and hung on us as though suspended on sticks. What mattered was that we were the proud owners and wearers of the Polish white eagle on our caps, similar to the one I had thrown into the snow so far away and long ago.

Up to now we had no contact with the British authorities, or anything British. Our only knowledge of that distant country was what we had learned at school. I remember well, in my early school days in Poland, looking at the world map and being greatly impressed by what I had seen. The map indicated different countries in different colours with pink dominating all the five continents. We were told the pink represented the British Empire, while a small island just outside Europe was Great Britain itself. How such a small island could control such vast lands my young mind could not comprehend. Maybe, I thought, the illustration of an Englishman I saw in the book had something to do with it. For the English gentleman was a person wearing black striped trouser suit, with a bowler hat and an umbrella. Connecting that knowledge with the event of the day, namely the British uniforms, our future, we thought, had never looked brighter.

For over a month we stayed in Wrevskoye. We ate better, we were getting fitter and our uniforms were slowly being filled up. During the day our superiors did their utmost to occupy our time. There were endless parades, marches, games and physical training, and occasionally we listened to talks on various subjects. Often we were reminded that we were the future generation of Poland where, they had no doubt, we would triumphantly return one day.

March, 1942, was the second anniversary of my exile. Such a lot had happened in those two years and a change in our fortunes, we hoped, was at last at hand. And so it came to be. Rumours began to circulate around the camp of our imminent evacuation to a neighbouring country. It mattered little to us what country as long as it was outside the Soviet Union. These were exciting days, more so when it became official. At that time we had no idea why Stalin allowed us to escape from his cruel grip.

Years later we understood why some of us were let free. There were two main reasons and both stemmed from the fact that the Red Army was on the verge of defeat. The fertile lands and most industrial areas were occupied by the Germans, Stalin badly needed help and friends. The Western powers provided both. Mostly through the efforts of Winston Churchill, the British Prime Minster, and the exiled Polish Government led by General Sikorski, the amnesty was agreed which resulted in our freedom. The other reason was mainly economic. The Soviet Union had no spare resources to feed, house and arm the growing Polish Army and the hundreds of thousands of Polish families who were now in the South. There remained one question to which I could never find a satisfactory answer – why only 7½% of Polish exiles were permitted to break the chains of the Communist yoke?

I do not know exactly why I was chosen for the job. Maybe because I was one of the elder boys, maybe because my handwriting was quite presentable. In any case the Company Sergeant instructed me to prepare a detailed list of all the boys under his command. Apart from the names, the list had to include other information such as date and place of birth, names of the parents, education, etc. In addition, the list had to be made out in two languages, Polish and Russian, and also in duplicate. Since there was no carbon paper, I had to write everything by hand and to top it all I was given a deadline. To complete my task I had to work hard, sometimes well into the night, but the necessary documents were ready in time.

Just before and during my writing I began having difficulties in swallowing my food. My throat became swollen and anyone looking at me could not fail to notice my discomfort. My Sergeant was no exception. In his opinion I had mumps and this, he said, if observed by the others, could prevent me making the long-awaited journey only a day or so away. The threat that I might again be left behind was something I simply could not accept. The Sergeant saw my shock, and suggested I wrap my neck up well and if asked why to say I had a sore throat. Taking his advice, I searched my belongings and selected a towel for that purpose. I covered my neck with the help of my friend and promised not to remove it until we had crossed the border.

The near miracle, the day we had all prayed for, arrived. At last we found out where we were going. Our immediate destination was Krasnovodsk, a town on the Caspian Sea some 800 miles away. From there we were to cross the sea to Iran, known as Persia at the time. Even at the eleventh hour the saying "I will believe it, when I see it" was widespread and understandable. Though the happiness of what was to come overtook our emotions, the plight of our families dampened our high spirits. Hardly a day would go by without my thoughts turning to their desperate struggle to live. I knew what they were going through. The guilt of not being able to help them, or even contact them, lay heavily on my conscience.

The warm days of spring were already with us as we travelled through the Kara Kum steppe. The train journey was long and exhausting in the crowded carriages. In a way I was glad there were so many of us as I was less noticeable with my wrapped neck. The fear of someone coming to me and saying I could not go any further had not left me. My fever and swollen throat prevented me from eating much, but I drank whatever I could get. I slept very little as we travelled through the night and, when morning came, our train stopped near the docks on the Caspian Sea.

23 March, 1942, was an ordinary day in the lives of many, yet to us, gathered there in Krasnovodsk, it was the day a nightmare was ending and a new life was beginning. We paraded outside the train and a short speech was delivered by the Officer in Charge. We would be marching, he said, in front of many Russian soldiers and officers supervising our departure. Now was our chance to hold our heads high and let them see that the two years of banishment and forced labour had not extinguished our Polish pride. On the orders of the Soviet officials, he concluded, we must surrender all our Russian documents and money. Before we marched off, each of us was given two very salted pickled herrings, as our food ration for the journey across the sea.

Never had our Company marched so smartly as across those last few hundreds of yards of Russian soil We could see the quayside crowded with uniforms of all kinds. By far the greatest number wore British battledress. But, of course there were the dreaded uniforms of the Red Army and the Soviet Police, guarding our passage to the boat. Slowly we walked down the gangway where our names were carefully checked against the lists in their possession and constantly reminded to hand over any documents or money. The boat on which we were embarking was a single-deck cargo ship and already looked overloaded. We were led towards the stern where we found enough room to sit down on the steel deck and rest.

Through that same gangway some 114,000 Polish men, women and children walked to freedom out of 1,500,000 Poles forcibly deported in 1940. The rest, even those who succeeded in reaching the South, were left behind. After the war only 850,000 returned to Poland and the vast majority of the remainder perished in the Soviet Union.

What were the thoughts of we young people on the boat when it sailed away? Certainly most of us gave thanks to God for our deliverance, but my exact thoughts are lost, mixed with the emotions of the moment. Now, after nearly half a century, if I had that day again, I would quietly pray for my dear mother who died only days after I left her. May she rest in peace. God help those who were left in the Soviet Union, and I include here the Russian people who deserved better. But forgive me for shouting at the top of my voice, "Damn you, Stalin, for creating the land where the cheapest commodity was a human life."

Epilogue

We landed at Pahlevi, the Caspian sea port town in Iran. We stayed there for a few days on the beaches, now in the hands of the British Forces. Then we were taken by lorry to Teheran aerodrome, where we spent a few weeks. While I was there I found out that my youngest sister was in an orphanage not far away. I went to see her, but she did not recognize me. In front of her I cried like a baby. From Teheran across the Syrian desert, again by lorry, we were taken to Palestine.

I spent two happy years in three camps: Bashet, Quastina and Barbara. We were cadets and trained as soldiers, resuming our interrupted education. There I met my elder sister, Lucia, who had joined the Polish Army. Through the Red Cross I was given the address of my father and younger sister Joanna. They were living in Isfahan, a town in the south of Iran, and from then on we kept in touch. There also, while standing in the cinema queue, I saw a little girl playing not far from me. I did not know it then, but much later that girl became my wife. In the middle of 1944 hundreds of boys, including myself and another boy who later married my sister Joanna, volunteered to join the Polish Air Force.

Via Egypt we sailed to Great Britain and landed in Liverpool. By train we were taken to Blackpool and billeted in bed and breakfast houses. Selected to serve as air crew, I was trained as an air gunner at RAF stations in England and Scotland. In May, 1945, my training completed, I went to

London on a fortnight's leave, where, with many others, I celebrated the end of the war.

In 1947, having served in the Italian campaign, my sister Lucia arrived in Great Britain. That year also my father, with Joanna and Jagoda, came to this country for a happy reunion in a camp near Cirencester. Later they moved to an old RAF station near Melton Mowbray where I joined them late in 1949, after my demobilization. Through the labour exchange, having had brief courses in building draughtsmanship, I was accepted as an office boy in an architect's firm in Nottingham where the incident I described in the Preface occurred.

Late in 1950 I was introduced at a dance to an attractive girl named Aleksandra Kwolek. She was the little girl I had seen in Palestine and we married in August, 1952. Her family lived in Aldridge, a little village outside Birmingham. We moved there the same year where I worked as a surveyor with a local brewery. In 1953 we were blessed with a lovely daughter and we named her Krysia. She eventually married a handsome Englishman, Barry Taylor. Now they have two good-looking and clever boys, Krystian and Johnothan, and an adorable girl named Imogen.

In 1955 the brewery appointed me as their surveyor, and later as architect to the South Wales Branch. Here, five years later, our son Christopher was born who grew up into a man we are very proud of, with a passion for music, but teaches mathematics.

As to the rest of my family, my father died in 1978, as did my sister Lucia a few years later, leaving two children. My younger sister Joanna married that boy who was in the same Company in Palestine, named Zenon Goralczyk. They had one daughter Bogusia, and are still living in Melton Mowbray. Jagoda, my youngest sister, married a Polish boy, Edek Wozniak. They have two children, Anette and Mark, and are now living in South Africa.

Lesia, my wife, and I, now in the twilight of our lives, now live in South Wales and are grateful to this country and its people for giving us refuge when we needed it so badly.